THE
TALKING CURE

MORTON M. HUNT and RENA CORMAN
with LOUIS R. ORMONT, Ph.D.

THE
TALKING CURE

A CONCISE AND PRACTICAL GUIDE TO
PSYCHOANALYSIS TODAY

With a Foreword by Leopold Bellak, M.D.

Harper & Row, Publishers New York, Evanston, and London

CONTENTS

v

FOREWORD

In our modern world of ever increasing specialization, the popularization of technical subjects has a constructive, even essential role to play. The best informed physician, engineer, or chemist finds those areas of science outside his own ken almost beyond his comprehension; the same is especially true of those in the humanities and nonscientific professions.

For unfortunately the specialist in one branch of science is almost never well equipped to explain his own work to nonspecialists, or to specialists in other areas. The job of translating professional jargon into the common tongue, of seeing perspectives rather than details, of anticipating the stumbling places and the informational gaps of the layman, requires science writers with special skills and talents which are as rare as they are needed. I believe the authors of *The Talking Cure* have successfully performed just such a service for psychoanalysis as a form of treatment. I do not agree with everything said in this book, but I need not agree with them fully to be able to recognize, and to assert, that they have done a very good job of making this much misunderstood and rather arcane subject readily comprehensible to all those who are outside it. Clarity and intellectual dignity have been brought to bear on the misunderstandings and questions which I have often heard voiced.

The Talking Cure is a good title, even though it is far from a complete title for psychoanalysis today. But the authors make this quite clear. In the time of "Anna O.," who coined the phrase "the talking cure" for the as yet unnamed therapy, psychoanalytic treatment was in its infancy, and was usually most concerned with catharsis and its airing of the unconscious. Freud soon became aware, however, that it took much more than the mere verbal relief of repressions to produce lasting cures. Indeed, what was needed was a complex process, carried on under expert guidance, which proved to be closer to a "thinking cure," or even better, a "re-thinking cure"—a process in which problems that baffle the child emotionally and intellectually are re-lived and re-examined as an adult, with the adult's developed intelligence and the expertise of the psychoanalyst collaborating to solve the problems and thus eliminate them as the source of irrational conflict. Yet more than re-thinking is involved; feeling is as important as thinking in the analytic process, which might therefore just as legitimately be called the "re-feeling cure." For all that, Anna O.'s phrase still has the ring of truth about it, for above all else, psychoanalysis proceeds through words—and seeks to cure.

Freud's basic contribution, it seems to me, was to establish the continuity between childhood and adulthood, between dream life and waking life, between health and illness, between the conscious and the unconscious processes. The multitude of differences of opinion among psychoanalysts (not different from the varied opinions in other healthy sciences) actually concern relatively minor issues—the details of the ways in which certain events in a person's life produce future effects, and the details of the therapeutic ways of altering those effects.

In this respect it has been useful for me to imagine that the child starts having all sorts of perceptions from the moment it is born. The adult we meet might then be compared to a complex composite of perceptions, not unlike a composite photograph of innumerable components. Certain contemporary perceptions are structured by past perceptions, sometimes excessively so: a certain past image of father or mother may unduly color one's perception of and reaction to authority figures, as if one were seeing through special kaleidoscopic eyeglasses. Some of these perceptions and reactions may be as obscure to the person concerned as the individual components of a photographic multiple exposure. Psychoanalytic treatment, then, is concerned with the resolution of contemporary perceptual distortions into their developmental components and a correction of the internalized lenses, as it were, when they are unduly distortive: the psychoanalytic process appears able to undo the effect of the past on the present. This, by itself, seems a unique phenomenon, as often life histories seem to develop with as much inevitability as a Greek drama.

The authors of this book wisely avoid getting embroiled in highly technical developments. They concentrate first on the broad contributions of psychoanalysis—its status as a general psychology, not only a psychology of the abnormal. They point out that not only classical psychoanalytic treatment can be derived from psychoanalytic theory, but that briefer forms of psychotherapy based on psychoanalytic dynamics have a valid place in the over-all mental health picture. And of course they spend the greater part of their time showing how general psychoanalytic theory is translated into day-by-day psychoanalytic treatment; while so doing they remain intelligently eclectic, without sacrificing sound basic principles.

These matters are more important to the literate and thinking public today than ever before. For psychoanalysis has given us knowledge and a framework of theory with which to understand those problems of human behavior which not only trouble individuals but weaken the structure of community life. Today, when people are concerned with the repair and strengthening of the structure of society, mental health is deservedly becoming a subject of intense concern, and of community-wide activity.

In this atmosphere—symbolized by President Kennedy's message on mental health legislation and the recent act of Congress to create community mental health centers—an understanding of psychoanalysis, psychoanalytic treatment, and of the theory on which it and most of the other modern therapeutic methods are drawn has become a must for every educated and thoughtful person. I believe that the present volume makes a valuable contribution toward this end.

LEOPOLD BELLAK, M.D.
Director of Psychiatry,
City Hospital Center
at Elmhurst, New York

November, 1963

AUTHORS' NOTE

We have chosen to offer this description of psychoanalysis in the form of a series of conversations between a psychoanalyst, two men (a lawyer and a teacher in an art school), and two women (a housewife with a teen-age son and an unmarried career girl), in the hope that the range of questions and doubts broached by such a variety of individuals may truly reflect our readers' concerns, and that therefore the explanations may be particularly useful to them. The material contained herein, although fictional in presentation, is based on extensive reading in the field and intensive interviews with psychoanalysts.

Among the many people who personally helped us in the preparation of this book, those to whom we owe special thanks include Robert T. Morse, M.D., of the American Psychiatric Association, Burness E. Moore, M.D., of the American Psychoanalytic Association, Arnold Bernstein, Ph.D., of the Council of Psychoanalytic Psychotherapists, and Jane D. Hildreth, of the American Psychological Association.

As knowledgeable readers will recognize, we have borrowed from people of diverse schools of thought—not in order to impose our own brand of eclectic psychoanalysis, but rather to piece together a good likeness of the theory and practice of present-day psychoanalysis, as it actually exists.

ABOUT THE TITLE

Scores, perhaps hundreds, of phrases have been coined over the decades to characterize psychoanalysis. Yet the best of them all, it seems to us, was the inspired creation of the very first patient treated by a technique preshadowing modern analysis. "Anna O.," whose case was chronicled long ago by Josef Breuer and Sigmund Freud, found that many of her serious symptoms got better after she uncovered, through talking to the doctor about them, how and when they first appeared and what emotionally hurtful events they had been connected with. We have delighted in borrowing as our title her own name for this process—"the talking cure."

THE
TALKING CURE

CHAPTER
ONE

TRUE OR FALSE?

*A few introductory facts and fallacies about psychoanalysis,
including: the stereotype of the analyst; psychoanalysis as the
destroyer of marriage; Freud and sex; falling in love with the
analyst; psychoanalysis versus time, religion, creativeness, and
morals; the expensive years; the use of drugs and hypnosis.*

TEACHER: Doctor, I've been wanting to ask you for some advice that was really asked of me. One of my colleagues at school, who had been a practicing homosexual, married a student of his about a year ago. They thought they were in love with each other, and he hopefully believed he could cut off his old ties and abandon his homosexual habits. But they've been having a lot of trouble and they are both afraid the marriage is falling apart. They want help, but they want help to keep them together. They're afraid to try psychoanalysis for fear it might break up the marriage completely.

PSYCHOANALYST: Why do they think analysis would break up their marriage?

CAREER GIRL: Oh, come now, Doctor! We've all known couples whose marriages ended on the rocks once they entrusted their troubles to an analyst.

PSYCHOANALYST: It's true that a number of marriages break up after one of the partners has been analyzed. But this usually happens when the marriage is built on unhealthy foundations—on the very sickness that finally brings the patient to the analyst. Most marriages, however, are *saved* by analysis and develop into bet-

1

ter relationships, because the patient is made to see that the anger and resentment he has been directing against his spouse are not really caused by her, but are the result of hidden tensions.

CAREER GIRL: Well, even if psychoanalysis doesn't always destroy a marriage, it certainly tears into a person's relationships with other people. I've known some garrulous types who've bored me to tears talking about their experiences with their analysts.

PSYCHOANALYST: Talking about one's analysis is not so frequent as all that. When it does occur—usually only early in the treatment, at that—it's because the patient is trying to dilute the painful emotions which are being aroused during his sessions. But this is only a phase—it passes.

LAWYER: And how about the people in analysis who are so absorbed in themselves that they have no time or concern for other people's problems?

PSYCHOANALYST: These individuals are trying to digest a lot of highly significant material. It takes time and energy, and of course they're absorbed. Actually, it rarely cuts off their real relationships or inhibits their social functioning. They're no more absorbed than an artist working on a painting. The artist's actions are more socially acceptable, that's all.

LAWYER: It's easy for you to be so tolerant. All you have to do is sit there where your patient can't see you, making little notes and dozing when you get too bored.

PSYCHOANALYST: That's the sort of myth about analysts that might drive me to drink if I didn't have a psychoanalyst's understanding of why people want to believe such things. Being an analyst is work—hard work. Simply to listen with total professional attention, hour after hour, is tough enough; and to deal effectively with the turbulent emotions being poured out is still tougher. I can assure you that we don't just sit there making notes or dozing. But by this time I should have thought such an idea might disappear, along with the stereotype of the beard and the Viennese accent.

HOUSEWIFE: It's obvious that *you* don't have a beard and an accent, but don't a lot of other analysts?

PSYCHOANALYST: It's true that a Freudian beard and a Viennese accent were standard equipment for a long time. After all, psychoanalysis was a very young science, and any strength which could be derived from an association with Freud was needed to disarm the suspicious public. But we are not Samsons, and today we feel completely adequate without a trace of a beard or a hint of old Vienna in our voice.

LAWYER: Now you're going to tell me you don't use a notebook either!

PSYCHOANALYST: Well, not very much. Most analysts do take a few notes from time to time, but most notes are made after the session is over, and even then few analysts keep really extensive notes.

LAWYER: Well, what do you do with the interval between patients?

PSYCHOANALYST: We use it to think over the events of the session just ended, to digest the significance of the subjects which were discussed, to put them into proper perspective in the light of what we have previously learned of the patient and his problems, and to make mental note of the meaningful points.

LAWYER: A *mental* note only, eh?

PSYCHOANALYST: For the most part, yes. Analysts are trained to rely on their memories, so that they can perceive the connection between phrases or acts which come to their attention on widely separate occasions. By the way, Freud himself didn't use a notebook at all. He believed it was more important to watch his patients for some revealing gesture or expression. In his *Collected Papers,* he remarks: "He that has eyes to see and ears to hear may convince himself that no mortal can keep a secret. If his lips are silent, he chatters with his fingertips; betrayal oozes out of him at every pore."

TEACHER: Hmmm, makes us poor mortals sound pretty weak.

PSYCHOANALYST: No, just understandable and accessible.

HOUSEWIFE: Speaking of Freud, is it true that he interpreted everything as part of a sex drive?

PSYCHOANALYST: You must remember that Freud was making his discoveries during the prudish, inhibited Victorian era; it isn't surprising that many of the people who came to him were disturbed primarily by hidden sexual feelings. We all know how strait-laced and unnatural the moral attitudes were in those days. Emotions and desires that today we recognize as quite normal were considered depraved then. Freud describes the case of a young woman who came to him for treatment of a severe depression. She had been devoted to her fiancé, but suddenly feelings of revulsion toward him developed, appearing at the same time as the onset of the melancholy. The cause was soon traced back to her fright over an embrace in which she could feel her fiancé's erect penis against her body, through both his and her clothing. Freud adds that such a sensation—or even the sight of the outlines of men's genitals through their clothes—was the source of a good many symptoms he saw in women. This kind of case is typical of that period; such reactions have virtually disappeared today.

HOUSEWIFE: Are you saying, then, that analysts today don't agree with Freud's belief that sexual desires cause all the trouble?

PSYCHOANALYST: We know today that emotional disturbances generally have more complex causes, which I'll go into more thoroughly at a later date. Psychoanalysis has naturally expanded and added to Freud's original theories as new situations posed questions for which there were no ready answers. But it's only fair to say that what Freud meant by "libido" or "love instinct" or "sex drive" was not so narrow and specific as his detractors say. Not only did he use the terms rather inconsistently, but he modified and added to his own propositions throughout his life, so that by his later years sex included the liking of the body for warm and pleasant contact, for affection between members of the family, for loving emotions, and for a constructive and positive drive toward acceptable social behavior. Freud's use of the term "sexuality" to include all these things is unfortunate, but we have no word that takes in the scope of his meaning.

LAWYER: If analysis is more than just getting rid of sexual repressions, how come the ladies are always falling in love with their analysts?

PSYCHOANALYST: It's true that at some point in their analyses patients may believe themselves in love with their analysts. But then at other times they hate them, too. I had one beautiful young redheaded patient who used to curse me up and down, in language worse than that of a dockside stevedore, sometimes with words I had never even heard before. It's part of the complicated relationship between the analyst and the patient, and basic to the analytic process. The romantic or passionate love feelings, however, are only temporary. A patient may think she's in love with her analyst for a while, but by the time the analysis has been completed, the Apollo-like visage has faded away, and though she continues to regard the analyst as a special kind of friend, she is able to recognize that he is merely a middle-aged, nondescript kind of fellow.

❦TEACHER: Could we return for a moment to my homosexual friend and his collapsing marriage? Do you think analysis would help him?

PSYCHOANALYST: I'm afraid I can't give you a flat answer. Some classical analysts follow Freud's belief that homosexuals are unable to become heterosexual through therapy. But many modern analysts believe that homosexuality arises from a variety of causes, and that, to some extent, there *can* be effective change depending on what factors are involved. There have now been a considerable number of cases in which homosexuals in treatment have altered their sexual habits, especially when they were bisexual to begin with, and unhappy about their continuing homosexual activities. And by the way, even those homosexuals who do not change their sexual patterns are often helped by analysis to function better in their work and get along better with the various people in their lives; they may still be homosexual, but not anxious or hostile. I wouldn't want to discourage your friend from getting help. Why don't you suggest that he see an analyst and discuss his own problem? There is at least the *chance* of success.

LAWYER: Well, well. So analysis isn't the magic cure-all after all.

PSYCHOANALYST: No one ever claimed it was. Its success depends on many factors, including the patient's desire to change and the nature of his illness. Analysis doesn't always help, but there are a host of fears and compulsions, feelings of anxiety and panic, and actual physical symptoms which can be alleviated by the understanding of yourself that comes through analysis.

HOUSEWIFE: Is this a kind of fear which can be helped? A friend of mine, who seems perfectly fine every other way, is afraid to cross the street by herself. If she doesn't have her car to get to a market with its own parking space, she has to shop at an expensive little grocery store down the street from her, on the same side of the block. Is that a case for analysis?

PSYCHOANALYST: Yes, agoraphobia, or, indeed, any morbid fear, is a common cause for seeking help through psychoanalysis; such fears are considered classic symptoms. But remember that they are only symptoms, not the disease. These fears act as outlets for a basic anxiety; they are self-deceptive devices to help the patient remain in ignorance of his real conflicts. And in analysis we don't deal primarily with the symptom, because if it is removed before the basic problem is discovered, the patient leaves and simply develops another, possibly more dangerous, symptom. We attempt, instead, to uncover and resolve the *cause* of the trouble. And when that goal is realized, the symptom appreciably lessens.

HOUSEWIFE: None of the people *I* know who've been analyzed had any obvious symptoms of that sort. How would they happen to go to an analyst?

PSYCHOANALYST: Actually, today most people come to analysis for broader reasons—because, for instance, they get no satisfaction from their jobs, or pleasure from living; because they can't form a stable, meaningful relationship with another person; because they get into fights with their employers no matter how many different jobs they try; and so on. These are less than obvious reasons, and such people do not always see their own problems clearly and seek analysis on their own. Often the suggestion that they try analysis comes from someone else, some friend or member of the family, perhaps. It's usually very much easier for another person to see that you are acting irrationally.

TEACHER: Doesn't the simple passage of time make analysis unnecessary?

PSYCHOANALYST: Sometimes. The human mind constantly attempts to bury the painful ideas which discomfort it, and very frequently succeeds in doing so. And Freud believed that there were some life experiences which could also "cure"—as, for example, when a submissive man is placed in a position of authority, is treated with respect, and "finds himself." But generally time doesn't heal an internal problem—it only encrusts it. And waiting for time to heal incapacitating feelings may be punishing yourself needlessly, delaying the living of a fuller, more satisfying life, and making possible treatment a longer, more difficult process.

HOUSEWIFE: But mightn't these feelings be due to temporary pressures, which pass away?

PSYCHOANALYST: Naturally, if external pressures are the real cause of tensions, and if they can be removed or adjusted to, then the tensions will disappear. A man might be having difficulty on his job, and be very upset about it. If his irritability and anxiety disappear when he changes his job, fine. But if he's in just as much trouble at the new job, and the one after that, and the one after that, it's only logical to assume that the problem is not with the job but with the man.

CAREER GIRL: Oh, I don't know. It seems to me that most jobs today *are* impossible, and that people are bound to be disturbed by them. In fact, I think the trouble with psychoanalysis is that it helps people adjust to a society that really shouldn't be put up with. A lot of people would probably be better off trying to correct society than learning to live with it.

PSYCHOANALYST: You're voicing a common criticism—namely, that analysis adjusts people to a sick society. But I don't think most analysts view their work that way. We feel that analysis, by removing a patient's neurotic rationalizations and fears, frees him to look about himself honestly and to use his capabilities in a constructive way to improve his lot and his world, without feeling unreasonably frustrated and personally defeated by events beyond his power to control.

HOUSEWIFE: Do you consider religious belief a "neurotic rationalization" that man must be freed of?

PSYCHOANALYST: Since many analysts—Karl Menninger, for instance—have strong religious beliefs, that obviously can't be a tenet of psychoanalytic theory, can it?

TEACHER: But wasn't Freud antireligious?

PSYCHOANALYST: Freud did feel that religion was based on an irrational faith, similar to and frequently substituting for the feeling a little child has toward his parents, and that a mature man shouldn't need such comfort. It was his position, of course, which gave psychoanalysis its notoriety as an enemy of religion. But today even Catholicism officially approves psychoanalysis. It is still true that if a patient's faith is based only on self-doubt or neurotic dependency, and if he clings blindly to a religion because it offers him a refuge, he may discard that faith when he has found a genuine belief in himself. But it is also true that he might develop a more meaningful faith, in keeping with his new values.

LAWYER: It still seems to me that analysis encourages a person to find a belief in himself at the expense of something or someone else. A friend of mine who was being analyzed while his wife was going to another analyst said then that it was like a war, with the husband and *his* analyst lined up against the wife and *her* analyst. Now why should that be?

PSYCHOANALYST: I doubt that it was. It's more likely that the husband and wife only *thought* their analysts were fighting their war.

TEACHER: Perhaps the idea would have been eliminated if they had both used the same analyst.

PSYCHOANALYST: Don't you think they might then have assumed that the analyst was taking sides? This often happens—which is one of the reasons why many analysts won't treat both husband and wife. There are other reasons, too, of course, involving problems of competitiveness and hostility and betrayal; and, indeed, these can present complications not only when husband and wife use the same analyst, but even when friends are being treated by the same doctor at the same time. One patient may be going through a period of smooth progress while the other is having a slow, painful time, and seeing that progress which the other person is making will only depress and confuse the troubled patient further. Freud treated both husband and wife at the same time, however, and some modern analysts feel quite capable of handling any problems which may arise under these circumstances.

LAWYER: I suppose they think they maintain fine judicial impartiality by their practice of saying nothing. Quite a technique! I can't help remembering what one Frenchman said (although he couldn't have been thinking of psychoanalysts, since he lived hundreds of years ago): "Silence is the wit of fools."

PSYCHOANALYST: Ah, but don't you remember what another Frenchman replied? "And one of the virtues of the wise!" But this is just another popular myth, this idea that all analysts say nothing and never *do* anything for their patients. There are many occasions when analysts speak up. It depends not only on the patient, and the phase of his treatment, but on the individual analyst. At one extreme are the analysts who rarely do anything beyond rephrasing the patient's questions. For instance, if the patient says, "Where am I going?" the analyst might say, "You're having difficulty deciding where to go." Orthodox Freudians say relatively little except at certain crucial junctures; the more "active" analyst will discuss and explore a problem with a patient. But in general, the analyst is not there to tell the patient what's wrong.

TEACHER: But why not? Why can't he be like a good teacher, who is able to explain things adequately to his students and to make them understand?

PSYCHOANALYST: The patient isn't a student, and telling him isn't sufficient to cure him. For a successful psychoanalysis, the analyst must help the patient dredge up from his unconscious hidden memories of his life, and re-evaluate the meaning of certain harmful childhood experiences. He must undergo what we call "emotional re-education." It's a slow and painful process, but it's the only way we know of at present to make a fundamental reconstruction of personality.

TEACHER: Isn't there a way to shorten the process? Like hypnosis? Or a drug like sodium pentothal or LSD?

PSYCHOANALYST: There are some analysts who use hypnoanalysis, narcosynthesis, or LSD therapy. And these methods do appear to speed up the revelation of the patient's problem. But there is a difference between the analyst's having the information and the patient's understanding the significance of it and being able to act on the knowledge. This is always the difficulty; and most analysts feel that the conscious and willing participation of the patient is, in the end, the most conducive to his understanding. Moreover, if the analyst perceives or extracts hidden material and presents it to the patient before the patient has slowly arrived at it himself, the effect may be disastrous.

Last year, for instance, a middle-aged woman was admitted to a mental hospital with which I'm associated; she was wild and totally confused, and had to be given a whole series of electroshock treatments to calm her. It developed that she had been going to a hypnotist because she had had amnesia, and he had been able to unearth some pretty sordid facts about her childhood. At the age of six, she had lived in a brothel, the madam of which was her own mother. Her twenty-year-old uncle used to come there and bribe the little girl with dolls and candy to engage in intimacies with him. When the hypnotist told her what he had learned, it was far too great a shock for her, and threw her into the violent state that sent her to the hospital. So you see, in addition to not helping, the knowledge procured from hypnosis can be downright dangerous. There are some situations where hypnosis is helpful, usually in short-term psychotherapy where temporary improvement is needed to accomplish a specific objective. But it has to be used with considerable discretion.

LAWYER: Isn't psychoanalysis itself pretty dangerous? I've heard that some people kill themselves because of it.

PSYCHOANALYST: Sometimes very depressed people prefer to try analysis rather than be hospitalized. Since depression is often caused by feelings of hostility which have been turned inward, the analyst tries to relieve it by bringing out these buried aggressions and turning them toward himself. But in rare cases, before the analyst succeeds in this aim, the depressed person may commit the ultimate act of aggression against himself—suicide. And infrequent though it is, it's a possibility that haunts every analyst who has such a patient. Psychoanalysis, in the wrong hands, *can* sometimes damage a personality, but it doesn't in itself exert enough influence to make anyone kill himself.

TEACHER: Is it influential enough, though, to help older people? My wife's uncle is considering analysis, but he's well past fifty. Do you think he's too old?

PSYCHOANALYST: There's no flat answer for that. One person of sixty is old, another is young at the same age. Analysts have worked successfully with many people in their fifties and sixties. It depends on the severity of their problems and the intensity of their motivation. But that is true of the young also.

HOUSEWIFE: How can you tell how severe the problem is or how intense the motivation? Do you have to treat a person for a while to find out if he's a good bet for your kind of help?

PSYCHOANALYST: It usually takes a few months to tell whether analysis can be useful, no matter how young or old the prospective patient. There are cases, of course, in which the individual quite clearly is not sufficiently motivated, or has symptoms which are not amenable to psychoanalysis, or where he requires hospitalization because he is too sick to be left unprotected. When this is the case, the patient or his family is advised of the more suitable course of action.

LAWYER: What about those rich women who think it's fashionable to go to an analyst? Do you ever turn them down?

PSYCHOANALYST: The fact that more people in one social class than in another seek analysis isn't proof that such treatment is unnecessary. Some cultural groups are simply more aware of the proper recourse for certain emotional troubles. If a patient does come to an analyst primarily because it's the thing to do, he soon drops out. The process is too unpleasant for anyone who isn't in real distress. One learns a great deal in analysis, and some of it is very hard to face. But I hasten to point out that when a patient has finally received his emotional re-education, he almost always feels that it was well worth it.

CAREER GIRL: When does he graduate, though? Some of my friends rush back to their analysts every time they run into trouble on their job.

PSYCHOANALYST: No one can foresee every trouble spot in his life. Analysis prepares a person as well as it can for the future; but unfortunately it isn't equally successful with everyone. And it's natural, isn't it, for an individual with an emotional ailment to go to a doctor, just as he would with a physical illness? But I assure you that this doesn't occur as often as you think. The successfully analyzed people simply go about their business and you never know they once had trouble.

TEACHER: Are those successfully analyzed people able to work in the same way? It's often said of the creative person, for example, that it is his very neurosis which produces his art. Won't he do less work or no work when he's not emotionally upset?

PSYCHOANALYST: Possibly the nature of his creative output would be somewhat altered. I can't, for instance, imagine Edgar Allan Poe writing exactly the same poems and stories if he had been analyzed. And many people have been concerned with the possibility you suggest. Erik Erikson, Professor of Human Development at Harvard, for instance, has concluded that "Genius as such can neither be explained nor treated away; only, at times, its delay and inhibition and its perversion to destructive or self-destructive ends." And analysts agree: they feel that, far from curtailing an artist's productivity, therapy frees the artist to work with much more facility and spontaneity, and to draw on far greater areas of his mind and experience.

LAWYER: Maybe so, but doesn't analysis also free a person from moral responsibility? I've heard that you can do no wrong in an analyst's eyes.

PSYCHOANALYST: It's true that psychoanalysis doesn't say, "Thou shall not." It has other business. Although a preoccupation with pornographic literature and sexual fantasies, for example, is no more acceptable to the analyst than to the clergyman, the analyst doesn't view such an obsession as a sign of immorality. He recognizes in it a symptom of mental illness. But this view of psychoanalysis as amoral is just another of the not-at-all surprising misconceptions you've proffered. I hope that in return I've been able to offer you at least a glimpse of the truths obscured behind these fallacies.

CHAPTER TWO

WHERE DOES
ANALYSIS FIT IN?

A brief survey of the range of mental illnesses; a panorama of the kinds of therapists and therapies, including self-help, ventilation and reassurance, pastoral and family counseling, deep forms of psychotherapy, physical therapies, and the techniques of mental hospitals.

PSYCHOANALYST: I'd like to talk about the way psychoanalysis is used against mental illness, and I ought by rights to begin at the very beginning, with a definition of such illness. (By the way, I am going to be using the term "mental illness" to refer to the whole range of psychological disorders, from total mental breakdown to minor maladjustments and emotional upsets. Some people use the terms "emotional illness" or "emotional disorder" to set off those psychological problems or disturbances which do not require hospitalization, but the President's Joint Commission on Mental Illness and Health, and many other professional people, prefer to use the one encompassing term.)

Defining the term, however, is very difficult to do in a simple, decisive way today. Oddly enough, for many centuries it *did* seem simple: a person was either normal or he was a maniac. Short of the berserk or the totally deranged, people with various degrees of psychological disorders were thought to be normal but eccentric, or unduly sensitive, or given to "melancholy," or something of the sort. But in recent decades we have learned so much about human behavior that we no longer draw a sharp line between the mentally ill and the mentally healthy. We know that there are

13

many different degrees of mental or emotional illness, with the fellow who thinks he's Napoleon at one extreme and at the other the man who, say, flies into a rage when his wife makes a mistake in her checkbook balance. I'm glad to say that we professionals don't find it necessary to draw simple boundaries any more, but can recognize the full extent and many varieties of psychological disturbances.

LAWYER: You're *glad* to say that? Glad to know so many of us are nutty?

PSYCHOANALYST: Please, I didn't say *that*. What I'm glad about is the fact that the recognition of the many gradations of mental illness, and the awareness of its presence in so many people, are beginning to remove the stigma of being "nutty," as you put it. People are beginning to realize that mental illness is not a dreadful and hopeless condition that sets the victim apart from normal human beings forever. They are beginning also to realize that it is better to be treated than to suffer and to justify one's sufferings; that it is no more ignoble to get help for frigidity than for rheumatism; and that one should be as free from shame in seeking treatment for a psychological ailment as for a germ-caused fever.

LAWYER: What's so great about thousands of people rushing to a head-shrinker because they don't have the strength of character to depend on themselves?

PSYCHOANALYST: You remind me of an old professor of mine who, when I was a young student many years ago, tried to dissuade me from becoming a psychoanalyst; he said I'd waste my life propping up weaklings. But that's an outmoded moralistic notion, and totally unscientific. A man with the grippe is neither a weakling nor unworthy of my time as a doctor simply because a virus proves stronger than his resistance. In the same way, a man whose built-in anxiety makes him frequently impotent with his wife is neither a moral weakling nor a nut, but a human being with a painful and crippling emotional disorder that requires and deserves professional treatment.

TEACHER: I can't help finding it frightening, nevertheless, to think that there are so many mentally ill people. I was shocked, for instance, to read in the papers some time ago about a mental

health survey in New York City which found that less than 20 percent of the people in a certain area were well!

PSYCHOANALYST: Were *completely* well, you mean. But don't
be too alarmed. Almost another 60 percent of those people had
such mild emotional disturbances that they were not considered in
need of help. You see their kind every day and live among them
all the time—henpecked men who turn for their satisfactions to
business, poor sports who insist on playing cards but are moody
and angry whenever they lose, young wives who get panicky during pregnancy, women who develop imaginary ailments during
the change-of-life transition, and so on and so on. The more important thing the New York survey showed was that about one-
fifth of the city population is psychologically sick enough to need
some sort of treatment, though three-quarters of these sick people
never get any. These untreated people are the ones who wage a
constant and often agonizing struggle with ailments which hamper and hurt them, but do not usually wholly incapacitate them—
ailments like impotence, inability to hold a job, compulsive
infidelity, persecution feelings, and many others.

LAWYER: I'd like to point out an inconsistency. First you
state that the line between mental health and illness can't be precisely drawn, but then you accept figures concerning how many
are or aren't well. You evidently do have some definitions, and
they're very far from the only one recognized in most courts:
M'Naghten's Rule of insanity, which says that if a prisoner has
a disease of the mind that makes him unable to tell right from
wrong, he cannot be held guilty of a crime, but that otherwise he
is sane and responsible for his actions. That's clear and simple,
and I like it.

PSYCHOANALYST: Unfortunately, it doesn't fit the facts of modern psychiatry. We know today, for instance, that the kind of bank
treasurer who systematically robs his own bank in order to indulge a passion for gambling is quite aware of right and wrong,
and cares what people think about him—but, in the grip of a neurotic need, he steals and cannot control himself. We know today,
moreover, that certain kinds of broken homes or disorganized
community life will tend to produce many persons who do know
right from wrong, but who totally lack a conscience. They simply

don't care what society thinks. And many judges today are coming to consider that these are forms of sickness and take it into consideration, especially when dealing with young criminals.

LAWYER: They certainly do, with the result that every time some young punk knifes an innocent old lady, his lawyer calls in a psychiatrist and tearfully tells the jury the boy couldn't help it. I suppose that's progress.

PSYCHOANALYST: Yes, it is! Maybe an occasional boy gets off who deserves punishment, but what is far more important is that the law is beginning to recognize that many of our actions are unconsciously motivated, and that a great deal of bad behavior cannot be corrected by punishment but only by the application of recent clinical knowledge of what makes people go wrong. Even so, the broadening legal conception of the mentally ill is still very narrow: it concerns only those who are dangerous to society. There are a great many more people who are neither "insane" in the legal sense nor "crazy" in a popular sense, but who do have milder forms of mental or emotional illness which affect their behavior and prevent them from living a healthy, normal, complete life.

CAREER GIRL: Wait a minute! As an old hand in the advertising game, I suspect the comparative that isn't compared to anything. "Milder," "more severe," "healthier," "sicker"—than whom? Who *is* mentally healthy, anyhow? And how do we recognize these paragons of perfection?

PSYCHOANALYST: *Touché!* You're demanding criteria by which one can judge mental health—and indeed there are such criteria. In general, I would say such a state is typified by the ability to live contentedly, to act in a socially acceptable way, and to set and to achieve one's goals within one's own capabilities. The mentally healthy person sees the world around him for what it is; he doesn't misinterpret, suspect, hate, or fear where there is no real cause. He solves his day-to-day problems in ways which are satisfying to him without being harmful to other people. He treats other people as individuals, tolerating them whether he likes them or not. He succeeds in his work and enjoys it; in fact, he enjoys the challenges of life as well as its securities. He's relatively free from depression, tension, and anxiety. He's flexible under stresses of personal loss, physical pain, illness, or the pressures exerted by those in authority. Above all, he can love. By that I mean he can partake of relationships with other people in which he recognizes their needs, understands their feelings, and cares about them enough to be made happy by giving them pleasure as well as by receiving satisfaction from them. He will be able to help his son to find his proper vocation, for instance, without imposing his own frustrated hopes on him. He will be able to take suggestions from his assistant and use them gratefully and give the younger man credit for them. He will enjoy seeing his wife in a new dress, but if they are short of money, he will be able to ask her—without a fight—to refrain from buying one.

HOUSEWIFE: You say "relatively free from tension," but what does that mean? Most of the women I know have days when they wished they had stayed in bed—days when the washer breaks down, when they keep tripping over the vacuum cleaner cord, when Junior comes in with a tear in his last decent shirt, until at last they end up screaming at their husbands the moment they walk in the door, and then bursting into tears. Is that excessive tension? Is that a kind of mental illness?

PSYCHOANALYST: Well, I could wish such women handled their problems a little more skillfully, but the picture you're painting is that of disturbance far below the borderline of mental or emotional illness. Every society—ours more than some others, perhaps—puts pressures upon people which produce some tensions and emotional difficulties. These are not the *inner* pressures, which cause the more severe and lasting kinds of emotional disorder, but external ones. The saleswoman caught between the buyer trying to unload end-of-the-season merchandise and the customer who's just looking may well get a splitting headache— and who can blame her? The bored assembly-line worker may go on a real bender once in a while. The young executive who has too big a house, too high a mortgage, too great a desire to get the next vice presidency, may get ulcer-like symptoms and insomnia.

CAREER GIRL: And the copywriter, with the account exec who's breathing down her neck, may break out in hives while she tries to knock out a scintillating sales pitch for cuticle cream.

PSYCHOANALYST: Yes, all such things—including the housewife's crying spells—are, in our world, relatively "normal" reactions to external stresses. Ordinarily people handle these reactions without professional help by backing off a little from the situation, or by staying with it and finding games, hobbies, political activity, or other outlets which dissolve the tension or give dignity to life or merely use up the anger. One woman I know told me, very perceptively, that she dreads the coming of snow, when her husband can't get out and smack the golfball around on weekends, because when he doesn't, he's a regular bear at home.

CAREER GIRL: So games and neighborhood politics can make us happier, healthier, and finer, too! You sound like one of those power-of-positive-thinking, self-help authors.

PSYCHOANALYST: All I am doing is pointing out certain obvious things that essentially well people can do to help themselves through the ordinary crises and strains of life. And obvious or not, these standard outlets and safeguards should all be tried instead of letting oneself drift into mental disorder.

LAWYER: Then you don't really think that every man who dislikes his job and every woman who yells at her kids should see a brain doctor?

PSYCHOANALYST: Of course not. The routine crises and pressures of our lives may produce emotional upsets in us, but usually they bear the same relationship to mental illness that bruises or colds do to serious physical diseases. We don't run to the doctor; instead, we take simple, appropriate actions and rapidly get better. But now let's take the next step. What if the simple, appropriate actions don't succeed? Take the case of a young girl in her sophomore year at college who is suffering from severe headaches and general nervousness. It's only proper that first her parents should have her see a physician and an eye doctor to look for some organic disorder. If none shows up to explain her troubles, they might next want to inquire whether she's eating the wrong kind of food at school, or not getting enough sleep. Each of these possible causes of her trouble could be handled externally, without assuming the girl needs psychiatric help. But if none of them is involved, and her headaches and nervousness remain a mystery, then she may require at least a kind of psychological first aid.

HOUSEWIFE: What on earth is that?

PSYCHOANALYST: I mean the shallowest or simplest level of treatment, which involves little more than a few searching discussions with someone generally aware of psychological problems and their causes, and able to help a person gain a little more perspective on herself and her behavior. The family doctor or the minister can often play such a part these days. Doctors are becoming increasingly knowledgeable concerning the extent and importance of psychologically caused ailments, and since they are figures of authority already, they can offer a good deal of comfort and direct advice without angering or frightening away the patient. The nervous college girl, for instance, might find out, after a thorough examination and a quiet chat with her doctor, that she feels anxious because she hasn't got a boyfriend, or because she's worried about her grades, or some such thing. And just the clear realization of such a factor may be enough to help her realign her thinking and her actions. In the same way, many young couples with marital problems, particularly those of love-making, are helped by doctors who can offer reassurance plus some specific advice as to technique, and effectively remove the feelings of shame or inadequacy that have made the young people awkward or unresponsive toward each other.

HOUSEWIFE: You also mentioned the clergyman. I don't mean to be irreverent, but why should a clergyman be considered competent to handle anything but questions of religion and morals? What can he do for someone with a real psychological problem?

PSYCHOANALYST: First of all, don't underestimate the power of listening, when it is done by a calm, disinterested, noncritical person—especially a person of importance and authority. During the Korean War, we found that soldiers who had collapsed with acute combat neurosis—"shell shock," as it was called long ago— could be salvaged and returned to duty in good shape in a few days if they were made immediately to talk out or "ventilate" their fears and their guilt feelings to a sympathetic, noncriticizing psychiatrist or medical aide. Afterward, the same system was put into effect for our troops stationed in Germany; there, men getting into trouble because of the emotional pressures of overseas assignment on a potential shooting front are encouraged to talk it out to chaplains, physicians, and sometimes even special noncoms who have been taught enough about the skills of listening and understanding to be adequate replacements for the more highly trained people. It has proved remarkably effective; the hospitalization rates for colitis, ulcer, and psychoneurosis all dropped sharply at the base hospitals after the system was installed.

TEACHER: Why do you call it ventilation? Isn't the process of relieving the problem by talking it out called catharsis?

PSYCHOANALYST: Yes, but I hesitated to use that word because for many well-read laymen it has acquired something of a magical connotation. Too many people think of the release of tension that catharsis gives as being a cure. Primarily, it yields a temporary relief. It isn't a cure of any fundamental disorder, any more than a good cry is a real cure to the barren woman who is unable to conceive. But in many cases, when an emotional disorder is the product of a specific limited crisis or a temporary traumatic situation, ventilation may be more than that. It may break the fever, so to speak, and permit the distressed person to muster his own forces once again, to summon up his own inner strengths, and to follow wise or helpful advice about the situation. And this is why the psychiatrically oriented minister can be effective not just on the battlefield of war, but on that of life, when illness or death or grave moral problems bring people to him in real psychological distress.

HOUSEWIFE: I still don't understand why a clergyman is equipped to do anything more than just sit and listen! Or is that all there is to it?

PSYCHOANALYST: No, that's only part of it. One must listen perceptively, hearing what lies beneath the spoken words. And one must reply skillfully, knowing which kinds of responses or questions will guide and help, and which will only frighten or anger the sufferer. Not every clergyman, unfortunately, is knowledgeable enough to do more good than harm. Indeed, *Action for Mental Health,* the final report to Congress by the Joint Commission for Mental Illness and Health, noted that, although more than a third of all the counseling problems brought to clergymen were estimated to be of serious psychiatric proportions, only one-tenth of them were actually referred to a psychiatrist. Nevertheless, the clergy is beginning to acquire professional skills. Perhaps nine thousand of the approximately 235,000 clergymen in the United States have had at least a modicum of professional training in this area, and pastoral counseling, which is what we call the use of psychological techniques by the clergy, is already well established. A number of hospitals and training institutes teach members of the clergy the fundamentals of personality structure and emotional disturbances, and there are about a hundred pastoral counseling clinics.

HOUSEWIFE: Still, I'm sure there are a lot of people who wouldn't feel comfortable discussing their personal problems with either their family doctor or a minister. What should they do?

PSYCHOANALYST: Probably the wisest thing to do, right from the beginning, would be to go to one of the more than three hundred good family agencies or sixteen hundred mental health clinics in this country, and talk to a casework counselor— that is, a social worker who does what is, in effect, psychotherapy. In fact, very often a doctor or clergyman will prefer to send a person to such an agency the moment he recognizes that the problem before him demands greater psychological knowledge and subtler therapeutic methods than he possesses. And this is all the more true if the problem is not shallow, or a matter of a passing crisis, but one of built-in personality traits—the *inner* pressures of which I was speaking previously.

HOUSEWIFE: But aren't clinics and family service agencies only for poor people?

PSYCHOANALYST: That's a common misconception, and quite untrue. These mental health clinics and family agencies offer their services to everyone, and base their charges on the patient's ability to pay. They are specifically designed to deal with simple to moderately severe emotional and mental disturbances, and have on their staff not only trained social workers, but clinical psychologists and consultant psychiatrists. And they are fully capable of deciding if the "client"—the caseworker's name for a patient—is beyond their capacity to help, and is in need of hospitalization, or physical therapy, or intensive psychoanalysis, in all of which cases these agencies are able to make intelligent and reliable referrals.*

HOUSEWIFE: My head is spinning—too many psycho-some-things. I never can get it straight! Psychologists, psychiatrists, psychotherapists, psychoanalysts—what are the differences? How do they all fit together—or don't they?

PSYCHOANALYST: Let me begin by defining psychology. Quite

---

* See Appendix A for more information about nonanalytic psychotherapists.

simply, it is the science of mental processes and behavior. It is the study of the mind in health as well as in sickness; it is concerned with intelligence and learning ability, perception and memory, education, emotions, special abilities, decision-making—I could go on and on. Any and every subject may be the province of a psychologist, who usually is studying or investigating it rather than primarily treating sick people, though sometimes he does that too, if he's also had that kind of training.

TEACHER: What is his basic training?

PSYCHOANALYST: The psychologist generally has a graduate academic degree—an M.A. or Ph.D., but not a medical degree. He is qualified by his degree and training to do scientific investigation in his field, including the testing of human beings. But unless he specialized in "clinical psychology" he is not automatically equipped to deal with people therapeutically. That takes special training and supervision.

TEACHER: You don't need much training to administer I.Q. tests, do you? Teachers do it all the time, routinely.

LAWYER: And I know many businesses give applicants aptitude tests.

PSYCHOANALYST: I was referring to tests of a much more interpretive kind—tests which reveal the major qualities, the real attitudes, and the hidden components of a man's personality. In these tests the significance of the answers, and the degree of abnormality or sickness present, are apparent only to the trained eye of the clinical psychologist. The Rorschach is one such test. The subject is shown a number of different ink blots, some colored, some just black and white, and asked what they resemble. What he sees or imagines in the blot tells a lot about him, but only to a qualified Rorschach interpreter.

HOUSEWIFE: We played a game like that when I was a child. We would drop ink into the fold of a piece of paper and press the ink out onto the rest of the sheet. Then when we opened the paper we would have a strange, but symmetrical design. It usually looked like a butterfly.

PSYCHOANALYST: *You* saw it as a butterfly, but other people might see many other things. To another person, one blot might seem like two waiters bowing to each other, or like an ugly elf, or like an old woman. To an abnormal person, every blot might resemble something alarming—a poisonous spider, for instance, or a devil with a pitchfork. In the same way, word-association tests can be very revealing. If the first word you think of when you hear "meat" is "potatoes," or "red," that's quite different from your first thinking of "cannibalism" or "kill." Again, Dr. Frederick Redlich at Yale has worked out a test based on reactions to cartoons and jokes. Take one by Charles Addams, for instance, which shows a homely middle-aged woman tied to a tree; her husband is placidly raking the autumn leaves into a great heap around her and preparing to burn them. Most people laugh at that, but individuals with deep-seated hostility—indeed, with repressed death wishes—toward their wives or mothers often say crossly that they see nothing funny about it at all.

HOUSEWIFE: All right, I think I understand about psychology now. What about psychiatry?

PSYCHOANALYST: Psychiatry is a *medical* science. Unlike psychology, which may be concerned with any and all aspects of behavior and mental processes, psychiatry is limited to the disorders of the mind and emotions, and their treatment.

HOUSEWIFE: Then are all psychiatrists M.D.'s?

PSYCHOANALYST: Right. A psychiatrist must first earn a medical degree, and then go on to specialize in psychiatry. As a specialist, he studies the origin and the diagnosis of mental ailments, and learns to treat them by prescribing drugs, hypnosis, shock treatment, psychotherapy, and occupational therapy, and administering some of these himself. He may do all of this as a hospital staff member, or in the public health service, or simply in private practice.

HOUSEWIFE: Didn't you just imply that psychotherapy was part of psychiatry? Yet I thought you said earlier that caseworkers and even some psychologists can give psychotherapy.

PSYCHOANALYST: It *is* confusing, isn't it? But look: psychotherapy is the psychological treatment of mental or emotional illness based primarily on verbal communication with the patient —discussions, probing, the search for self-understanding—as distinct from therapies which use drugs or other physical methods. Because that is so, the non-M.D. may use psychotherapy, if he has been trained to. So a psychotherapist can be a social worker, clinical psychologist, pastoral counselor, or psychiatrist. But only the psychiatrist can use drugs or shock treatment as well as psychotherapy.

TEACHER: Your definition of psychotherapy sounds to me just like a definition of psychoanalysis.

PSYCHOANALYST: Quite right! Psychoanalysis is *one* of the techniques of psychotherapy—the deepest-probing and potentially the most reshaping one, and particularly effective against certain classes of illness. But let me put that off for a while; I want to explain another point or two about psychotherapy in general.

CAREER GIRL: I certainly wish you would. I've heard that term applied to marriage counseling, voodoo, and some dear friend's advice to count to ten before screaming my head off.

PSYCHOANALYST: It's somewhat in the same position as mental illness. There is no single definition of it that is accepted by all schools or universally recognized.

LAWYER: That's why there are so many quacks in the business.

PSYCHOANALYST: Agreed. Reputable professional associations, however, are trying to set up adequate standards and have them legalized. But the whole field is very new and all this takes a good deal of time, you must remember.

CAREER GIRL: Well, what most usually takes place in psychotherapy?

PSYCHOANALYST: I would say that all good psychotherapy starts with the establishing of a warm, supporting atmosphere, in which the therapist is the sympathetic, understanding, nonjudging listener, who helps the patient to talk about himself without fear of blame or punishment, guides his thinking about his problems, and assists him in gaining an insight into their nature and in finding a solution to them.

HOUSEWIFE: How does the therapist do that?

PSYCHOANALYST: There are many different techniques, though they can be grouped generally in three somewhat overlapping classes. At one end is "simple, nontechnical psychotherapy," which deals primarily with problems and conflicts which arise from external situations and are dealt with consciously. This is what the doctor, minister, teacher, or vocational counselor practices when he gives common-sense, sympathetic counsel, encouragement, instruction, or distraction. Even marriage counselors and social workers sometimes fit into this category. But for any of these people to be of use to the patient, the latter must have a large degree of rational, conscious self-control; otherwise, this kind of support and advice is not really helpful.

TEACHER: You're suggesting, I take it, that the patient who can benefit from such help isn't very sick.

PSYCHOANALYST: Yes, I am. Indeed, where such counseling succeeds, you may be fairly sure that the trouble was caused predominantly by external stresses rather than by inner, or unconscious, forces, or what is sometimes called "intrapsychic conflict."

CAREER GIRL: I know a story that seems to prove your point. A gal I worked with, a whiz with an advertising slogan, was absolutely miserable with her husband—used to cry into her coffee telling me her troubles. She finally went to a marriage counselor with him, and after months of whatever kind of soul-searching goes on, she decided to get a divorce. I remember sneering at the spectacle of a marriage counselor whose professional efforts led to a divorce, but it was the right idea for her. She's remarried, and she's blooming. In fact, she's writing a book about how second marriages can succeed. The husband had been the really disturbed one, and he's still seeing a psychoanalyst.

HOUSEWIFE: But aren't marriage counselors and social workers trained to do more than just offer advice like trusted friends?

PSYCHOANALYST: A good many are. Many of them have had further training by psychiatrists or psychoanalysts, and practice the second category of psychotherapy.

TEACHER: What's that?

PSYCHOANALYST: It is sometimes referred to as "palliative or reparative psychotherapy." Here the therapist is aware of the effect of the unconscious forces in his patient's life, and takes them into consideration in dealing with symptoms, but makes no effort to impart this awareness to the patient. The social work counselor who skillfully interviews an argumentative housewife may come to understand her embattled relationships with her neighbors and her family. He may recognize the pseudomasculinity that haunts this woman, and may discover the cause in the woman's childhood—perhaps years of being alternately fussed over and repulsed by a capricious mother and ignored by a weakling father. But the social worker won't attempt to explain these causes to her, because he knows that the woman can't and won't accept them.

LAWYER: Why not?

PSYCHOANALYST: As I told you last week, "telling" such a patient can't remove the barriers which her unconscious needs have erected against her understanding, and it may only upset her terribly.

LAWYER: Then what will the therapist do?

PSYCHOANALYST: Without making her see the unconscious reasons, he will try to get her to see herself more clearly as she is. He will try to make her see that she is being unreasonably angry and vindictive in all her actions; that her poor, confused children are suffering from slaps unjustly administered; and that her husband is likely to try to prove his manliness with some other woman. He will encourage her to air her difficulties; he will make her feel like a worthwhile person who has valuable opinions and feelings; and perhaps he will suggest some specific measure, such as an extracurricular activity like building sets for the PTA play, where she can have physical action and variety, and a little opportunity to order people around.

LAWYER: How do you know that would work?

PSYCHOANALYST: Since the case is wholly hypothetical, I don't. But I know of a similar one, which was told me by Dr. Erich Lindemann, the psychiatrist-in-chief of Massachusetts General Hospital, in connection with clinical work he was doing there a number of years ago. A woman came to him who was having a great deal of trouble in her family life. She was an intelligent, dynamic person, with a job as an advertising copywriter for a department store. Unfortunately, she had a great need to domineer and exert authority, and she so ruled the roost in her domestic affairs that she had succeeded in making her husband impotent and her adolescent son nervous and withdrawn. Dr. Lindemann soon ascertained the unconscious motives that drove her into those paths so harmful to herself and her family, but she was unwilling to undergo psychoanalysis—which was the only way she could have come to grips with the reasons for her aggressiveness—so he contented himself with manipulating her life in an external fashion. He influenced her to ask for a transfer to the job of floorwalker in the store. Here all her top-sergeant qualities were put to good use: she performed her bossy job with exceptional zeal and skill, and after needling lazy stock boys and telling off slipshod salespeople all day, she was able to relax at home and be a warm, loving wife and mother. The husband gradually became a man again, and the son improved a good deal, too. Dr. Lindemann agreed, of course, that he had made no deep-seated change in her personality, and that if she ever lost the job, the old problems might reappear, but there is no question that he was able to help her and the people closest to her.

TEACHER: Isn't it possible that these so-called deep-seated needs would be so satisfied by the job that they would no longer be a problem to her? And that she would gradually crack her whip less even at work?

PSYCHOANALYST: Unfortunately, deeply rooted symptoms and traits are rarely relieved by such maneuvers alone. Usually, they have to be traced to the childhood experiences which have sensitized the patient to his current problems. But I don't want to underemphasize the importance of palliative or reparative psychotherapy, or of the value of "directive" or manipulative techniques. They are very valuable for those patients who don't have the time or the money for intensive treatment, or those who live too far from anyone equipped to give deeper therapy. Indeed, the largest number of people getting help for emotional ills must content themselves with these forms of psychotherapy. Some 450,000 people are helped by mental health clinics each year, and even more by family service agencies. But there are so few psychoanalysts in this country that only a relatively small number of patients can be in analysis at any given time—possibly only a tenth or a twentieth the number of those being helped by the briefer forms of psychotherapy.

LAWYER: How many people are treated successfully by these briefer forms of psychotherapy?

PSYCHOANALYST: Well, the very shallow type of so-called psychotherapy which I placed in the first category is for the most part so informally done, and with such borderline cases, that there couldn't be any figures on it. But for somewhat more seriously troubled people who seek social work counseling and reparative therapy, reports indicate that about two-thirds show improvement; although, as I suggested, the reparative technique is less likely to produce long-lasting effects. For more extensive structural changes in the personality, and for a number of serious neurotic ailments, it is necessary to have thorough reconstructive psychotherapy.

HOUSEWIFE: The third category?

PSYCHOANALYST: Exactly. That is what psychoanalysis is, and it is a far lengthier process.

TEACHER: Why?

PSYCHOANALYST: It is psychoanalysis, through the special techniques it has developed, which attempts to trace back the causes of present emotions and behavior to earlier buried conflicts of which the patient is unaware, and to uncover and modify these deeply rooted, unconscious, psychological forces which are causing the patient's suffering.

LAWYER: Why does that take longer?

PSYCHOANALYST: Because there are powerful, unconscious resistances to admitting the sources of the behavior, or to changing it. I'll go into all of this more thoroughly at a future time, but for now let me just remind you of the futility of reasoning with the man who's filled with panic when he has to sit in the upper balcony of a theater or with a woman who wears gloves constantly to avoid a possible contact with germs. The recognition of these irrational fears has become so widespread, in fact, that a little while ago I read a newspaper article describing how acrophobia sufferers who balk at crossing the Delaware Memorial Bridge, which rises 187 feet above the water, are routinely supplied with police-chauffeurs to take them to the other side.

LAWYER: All right, I think I've got that part fairly straight. But you say the psychoanalyst practices psychotherapy, and that the psychiatrist *may* practice it. Does that mean that the psychiatrist is a psychoanalyst?

PSYCHOANALYST: Not necessarily. Psychiatrists aren't analysts unless, in addition to studying psychiatry, they've studied analysis. Conversely, the psychoanalyst may or may not be a psychiatrist. He may have either an M.D. or a Ph.D., or sometimes only a master's degree, before he begins his analytic education, which involves several years of training at a recognized psychoanalytic institute. Besides this, he must undergo psychoanalysis himself, and must have worked with a number of his own patients while under the supervision of a control analyst, before he is officially accredited by membership in a professional association.

LAWYER: It sounds like a long way to go to earn a living!

PSYCHOANALYST: I quite agree. Maybe you have to be a little nutty, as you would put it, to begin with.

LAWYER: I withdraw the term! Peace!

TEACHER: How about the people who can't be helped by psychotherapy, analytic or not?

PSYCHOANALYST: Unfortunately, it is true that there are a great many people today who aren't able to, or who don't want to, cooperate in the psychotherapeutic relationship—and especially in analysis there has to be a great desire on the part of the patient to get well, surprising as that may seem to you. Moreover, when people succumb to a psychosis—schizophrenia, for instance, or melancholia—they have so profound a disorganization of the personality that they can't usually be reached by verbal techniques, and have to be hospitalized. For example, a woman may suffer from such severe depression during menopause that her family is afraid she might attempt suicide, a harassed workingman may suddenly be driven wild by imaginary voices, a meek choirboy may run amok and begin shooting at passers-by with his air rifle, an adolescent girl may become so withdrawn that she ceases to recognize her own parents. Such people need hospitalization, you can see; in the United States over 300,000 people every year enter mental hospitals. Luckily, much more is known about mental illness today than a generation or two ago, so diagnoses can be made quickly and accurately, and treatment can be begun at once—and we have found that the quickness with which it begins nowadays makes it remarkably more effective.

HOUSEWIFE: What kind of treatment is used?

PSYCHOANALYST: A mental hospital, or the special psychiatric wing of a general hospital, has a number of therapies at its disposal. Shock treatments are very effective for certain patients— primarily people in deep depressions; and tranquilizers and other new drugs, though they admittedly do not automatically "cure" the patient, have had a large share in the increasing number of discharges from hospitals. Then psychiatric social workers visit the patients, offer reassurance, psychotherapeutic aid when it can be used, and often see the patient's family, too. Psychiatric nurses understand the patients' ailments and can give proper, helpful service and make useful reports. There are all kinds of recreational facilities, from jigsaw puzzles and television to athletic fields, and occupational therapists oversee weaving, painting, carpentry, or whatever the psychiatrists in charge might prescribe. All these things help. And clinical psychologists give the tests about which we spoke before, and so reinforce the diagnoses and estimates of progress which are made by direct observation. Then when these mentally ill people have recovered sufficiently to be treated outside of the hospital environment, if it is at all feasible, they are released.

TEACHER: You said the number of discharges from hospitals is increasing. Do you mean proportionate to the number of admissions?

PSYCHOANALYST: Yes. Consider Pilgrim State Hospital in New York, which has fourteen thousand patients and is thus the world's largest mental institution. Newly admitted patients there—excluding the senile—have a four-out-of-five chance of getting out again, sooner or later, and most of them actually leave in less than six months. That's why mental hospital populations are decreasing, despite rising admission rates.

LAWYER: Psychoanalysis has no place in a mental hospital, has it?

PSYCHOANALYST: As a matter of fact, it has. You see, psychoanalysis has three different aspects. It is a particular type of psychotherapy used for the treatment of a variety of mental ills; it is a body of knowledge about, and a theory of, human behavior; and it is a method of investigation and further increase of psychological knowledge. As therapy it isn't particularly efficacious with the psychotic patients in a mental hospital, because it must have the conscious, rational help of the patient. Besides, it requires a great deal of the doctor's time, and in most mental hospitals each doctor can spare only a few minutes or so per patient per week. Analysts are used, however, in some hospitals, with some patients, even if only for reparative therapy. But it is as a *theory* that psychoanalysis has had the greatest influence. Not only have hospitals and mental health clinics been affected, but the understanding and treatment of every form of mental illness have burgeoned because of it, and the methods of all the practitioners we've mentioned have felt the unique force of its conceptions.

CHAPTER THREE

THE POTENTIAL PATIENT

*What's wrong with being neurotic; major neuroses and their
symptoms; character disorders, including perversions and ad-
dictions; major psychoses; who can be treated by psychoanalysis.*

PSYCHOANALYST: In order to tell you who can benefit from
psychoanalysis, and why, I think you have to know what causes a
psychological disturbance of any kind. And it will be helpful, too,
for you to know more about the different types of mental illness,
and the symptoms by which they are recognized. And, by the
way, it was psychoanalysis which played an enormous part in
revealing all this information.

You recall that we described the normal, healthy individual as
a man who was able to maintain a balance in his relationships
with the world. This balance exists when the conscious forces of
the mind dominate the unconscious. The mentally ill can't maintain that equilibrium; the unconscious processes are too strong.
The imbalance may be anywhere from little to great, resulting in
minor to major neuroses, or it may be so extensive that the unconscious forces dominate the mind completely, and you have a
psychosis.

Let us talk about the neurotic patient first. His illness may be
such as to make him quite ineffectual at work; or he may be demanding and possessive and hard to get along with; or it may
result in his being hysterical or jealous or depressed. He will certainly be uncontrollably self-centered.

TEACHER: Is everyone who's self-centered neurotic?

PSYCHOANALYST: No. Interestingly enough, any human trait,

any human act or thought or feeling can be either normal or neurotic or both. The philanthropist who sets up a fund to help the needy is normal, at least on the face of it, but the saint who gives up all his earthly possessions and leaves his family in poverty is acting from some unconscious need of his own.

HOUSEWIFE: Why is it so important whether an act is conscious or unconscious if it's useful?

PSYCHOANALYST: The personality which is moved by conscious processes is able to adapt to external realities and to learn from experience. It can be influenced by argument and logic, by success or failure, by rewards or punishment. To the extent to which our lives are governed by our conscious decisions, we are free. But when our decisions are guided by unconscious processes, they can't be reached either by reason or hope of reward. Furthermore, unconscious motives blindly drive us toward unknown goals which we can never attain, and, like Sisyphus rolling his rock uphill, the neurotic in pursuit of an unconscious and impossible goal is forced to repeat his efforts endlessly, regardless of his resulting unhappiness. The more a man's behavior is driven by unconscious forces, the less he learns from experience; the less he can develop or change, the less he is free and the more he is enslaved.

TEACHER: Why do we have unconscious forces, and why should their operation be so powerful?

PSYCHOANALYST: Let me try to explain it. A healthy personality is like a democratic state in which there are all kinds of private needs and conflicting interests, but in which things run fairly smoothly through mediation and compromise. The personality must reckon with its own sometimes opposing needs and desires as well as with its conflicts with the environment. If it's healthy, it compromises by giving as much satisfaction as possible to each contestant. But in every human being there are some desires, especially certain of those appearing in early childhood, which present unbearable conflicts. These must be suppressed, just as a traitor is imprisoned by the state lest he destroy it. Such impulses are buried in the unconscious, but they don't always stay safely buried. Instead, within the unconscious they are apt to exercise a powerful though unrecognized influence on us. These buried ideas and feelings are held down by a process called repression—a special kind of purposeful forgetting. As long as these ideas are repressed, they may exert pressures which find indirect—or neurotic—expression.

HOUSEWIFE: Could you give us an example?

PSYCHOANALYST: Consider the child who is angry with his mother because she pays attention to the new baby, and who hates the infant because it has robbed him of that attention. He needs his mother and wants her love, and so he must bury his anger. And when his mother tells him he must love the new baby, the need to please his mother causes him to repress the hatred toward his sibling, too. But then this boy, who has been toilet-trained for years, suddenly begins wetting his bed night after night. In this way his unconscious reveals his desire to replace the new baby and get the same attention, and at the same time it gets even with his mother by an act she finds annoying and troublesome.

HOUSEWIFE: Are you saying that even children can be neurotic?

PSYCHOANALYST: Well, a certain amount of neurotic behavior is inevitably involved in growing up. We're all aware of the neurotic episodes which occur in every childhood, even though we don't label them as such: nightmares, stereotyped behavior habits —such as the child who can't eat without his special fork—exaggerated loves and hates, blind rebellion and equally blind submissiveness, and food phobias, as well as bed-wetting.

CAREER GIRL: But children live so completely for themselves, and can't be rational the way adults are—I'd think that they must have to suppress *many* desires that are simply impossible, or intolerable to the Big People around them.

PSYCHOANALYST: Yes, every child represses some feelings. It's part of the growing-up process in civilization.

CAREER GIRL: Well, if everyone has repressed impulses, why isn't everyone neurotic?

PSYCHOANALYST: At the beginning of the Freudian era, when the origin of repressions was discovered to be in childhood events, such early experiences *were* considered the only cause and hence a theory of universal neurosis was plausible. But we know now that there are other factors that enter into the formation of a neurosis, factors which lend power to the unconscious forces born of buried desires. We recognize the importance of heredity, as well as the effects of the difficulties encountered in life. Some individuals are constitutionally stronger and better able to withstand the pressures of the unconscious. Others develop vulnerable spots, sensitized areas, which may lead to neurosis if other influences develop later. War, for instance, horrible as it is, results in neurotic symptoms for only some people. And some may have weak spots which collapse under the average vicissitudes of life.

TEACHER: Then anyone, anywhere, may become neurotic.

PSYCHOANALYST: Yes, the neurotic process can be found in all economic, intellectual, and cultural strata, in urban and rural life, in highly civilized countries as well as primitive ones. But though your genes and chromosomes may be the seat of trouble, and though your job and fallout and togetherness or the lack of it may be significant influences, the *sine qua non*, the absolutely necessary condition without which there can be no neurosis, is repression and its possibly hurtful effect on behavior.

TEACHER: In a normal person, do these repressions show no effect?

PSYCHOANALYST: Far from it. As I said before, our lives consist of an unstable equilibrium between the conscious and unconscious processes, and are shaped by them both. In fact, our characters are partially molded in this fashion. The way we eat, work, make love, and bring up our children, our economic goals, our morals, how we react to success and failure—all these are influenced to some extent by the unconscious forces of our personality. More, our choice of profession, of a wife, of companions, is forged in the struggle between these forces.

HOUSEWIFE: Let me see if I understand. You say that each of us, raised as most children are, represses a certain number of ideas and desires—

CAREER GIRL: Such as wishing Mommy would die so she can have Daddy all to herself?

PSYCHOANALYST: Yes, and anger when her father didn't bring her the doll he promised her, or her mother went away for a weekend and left her behind, or her sister had a beautiful pink dress on which everyone lavished praise, and of which she herself was most envious. Innumerable feelings and memories are repressed and leave their mark in reactions which can't be termed neurotic.

HOUSEWIFE: Then with all our repressions, we may still grow up and fall in love and marry and not have a neurosis at all.

PSYCHOANALYST: That's right. You may be particularly nice to old ladies, and dislike pink, and lavish toys on your own children, however. These are some of the ways our unconscious processes shape our character. Some people, however, may have a hereditary predisposition which makes it more difficult for them to recover from the effects of repression. They walk a thinner line, and if something unfortunate happens to them—

CAREER GIRL: Like being jilted?

PSYCHOANALYST: Possibly—or having a miscarriage or just working day after day for a difficult employer—almost any distressing situation which could be handled by a stronger person will be overwhelming to those who are so predisposed. Then, of course, there are those people who are not raised "as most children are," but are brought up by very strict or cruel or strait-laced parents. They would have had to repress so many more impulses that they would be particularly vulnerable to a neurosis.

TEACHER: How might such people act? What would they do that would indicate that they're neurotic?

PSYCHOANALYST: They might behave in a number of different ways. But there is one characteristic which most neurotic acts have in common: They appear to be less rationally motivated than normal acts. This is often clear to the patients as well as to observers. For instance, fear in a dangerous situation is rational, but breaking out in a cold sweat because of being in a crowded movie is not. Grief over the death of one's parent is rational; profound depression because your husband had to work late and couldn't take you dancing is not. Even more irrational is the depression which comes over someone after he has had some big success, like an important promotion. Obsessional fantasies of strangling one's children are obviously irrational. So are the rituals of constant hand-washing and overly precise orderliness which some people find themselves involved in.

TEACHER: I've heard a good deal about washing rituals. They're compulsions, aren't they?

PSYCHOANALYST: Yes. Compulsions are one of the major groups of neuroses. And one of the more clear-cut. There are really too many neurotic symptoms, many of them overlapping, for any classification. But as I said, the compulsives make up a large number. These include not only the handwashers and the ones with fantastic ceremonies which must be performed before getting into bed, but also the terribly neat people who become upset if one object in their drawers is out of place, or the very precise ones with strict rules of behavior.

LAWYER: These things don't sound so bad to me. The people you mention are probably all upstanding members of society.

PSYCHOANALYST: No doubt. But the feelings of panic and anxiety which arise when a well-developed compulsion is interfered with in some detail are impossible for a nonsufferer to imagine. The pain is such that compulsives will go to elaborate lengths, at whatever the cost to themselves, to perform their acts.

Dr. Theodor Reik describes a man who felt compelled to stamp the ground with his right foot whenever he entered a room or crossed an important line. This need was so great that he had gotten into the habit of planning ahead to meet it whenever necessary. On one occasion he was to drive a young lady to a neighboring city, through an area with which he was unfamiliar. He knew that when he crossed the city boundary he would have to make his gesture, and he not only had to be sure of the exact spot, but he had also to arrange an excuse for the gesture. So he arranged, on a subterfuge, for his chauffeur to drive him to the place the day before, and by constant questioning he managed to ascertain the boundary line in time to alight from the car, make careful note of his surroundings, and stamp his foot several times on the pretext of its having gone to sleep. Then during the trip with the girl, he managed to lead the conversation to the point where he could sing an appropriate song and beat time to it with his right foot when they approached the city line. You can see how many hours and how much energy must have been taken up in this man's life by this senseless need.

HOUSEWIFE: I've heard the term "obsessive-compulsive." Does that mean that the person who is compulsive is obsessed with the need to perform the act?

PSYCHOANALYST: Yes, sometimes. But often the term refers to the asocial ideas which frequently plague the minds of compulsive people, such as visions of hitting strangers, or killing near relatives, or having incestuous intercourse. Obsessional ideas may occur alone as well. They appear to have no relation to a person's problems, and are never actually carried out. I read a description of one case in which a man suffered from the obsession of wanting to hit people on the head with an ax. At first he was bothered very little by the idea, but he did avoid hardware shops. Later any object even slightly resembling an ax made him feel this same desire and the anxiety that went with it, until he even dreaded reading because the capital "L" reminded him of an ax. Naturally, even his professional life was affected.

CAREER GIRL: What causes such ideas?

PSYCHOANALYST: They are usually quite undisguised repressed infantile impulses. This poor fellow, after suffering twenty-five years with his obsession, went into analysis, where he discovered a more than usually clear-cut cause for his trouble. He had been jealous of his older brother, and had developed feelings of guilt as a result. Then when he was six, and was digging potatoes with a friend, he accidentally hit him on the head with his hoe so that the friend fell bleeding. He was afraid that he had killed the boy, and immediately developed severe guilt feelings, since to his unconscious mind the action represented the hostility he bore toward his brother.

CAREER GIRL: That's pretty pat. It sounds like a Hollywood script with Dr. Ingrid Bergman and patient Gregory Peck, who's cured during a long weekend.

PSYCHOANALYST: I said it was unusually obvious. But repressed childish desires are consistently present in obsessional ideas, even though the connections are usually harder to find.

HOUSEWIFE: Are repressed feelings as clear in other neuroses?

PSYCHOANALYST: Not in all, but in phobias, another group, the connection with childhood fears is usually quite clear. People with phobias are trying unconsciously to concentrate the anxiety and pain they feel from both the present difficulty and the past repression into a symbolic fear—the phobia—and then by avoiding the phobic situation, they hope to avoid the intolerable anxiety which the forbidden impulses produce. Thus the phobia often has an unconscious symbolic meaning.

For instance, a young boy may be very jealous of his older brother, and long to outdo him, to receive greater praise from his mother, even to harm the brother perhaps, so that he can be "king of the mountain." These desires have to be repressed in order that he be considered a "good boy" and "*so* fond of his brother" by his mother, and this ambition to be on top remains surrounded by feelings of guilt. Thus the anxiety evoked by an effort to compete with anyone, even as an adult, causes him to develop acrophobia —a fear of heights. Of course, the exact meaning of the phobia is not immediately evident, but has to be discovered in each case.

TEACHER: Would it be fair to say, then, that a phobia works in the opposite way from a compulsion, but toward the same end? A positive act performed to relieve anxiety is a compulsion, and a negative one is a phobia.

PSYCHOANALYST: Excellently put! The phobia attempts to alleviate anxiety by avoiding the symbolic cause, whereas the compulsion tries to propitiate the tension by ritual, and the obses- sion attempts to exorcise the painful feelings by exposing—in a distorted fashion—the repressed wish. There is another interesting category of neuroses, hysterical conversion, in which the patient tries to relieve his anxiety by substituting a bodily symptom for unacceptable unconscious impulses. Thus the repressed wish can be expressed and at the same time rejected.

HOUSEWIFE: What are these substitute symptoms?

PSYCHOANALYST: An hysteric might display paralysis of a limb, convulsive spasms, dumbness, deafness, blindness, or selective amnesia. But there is no organic disease involved.

TEACHER: We had a case of that description in school. One of the students became temporarily blind before a final exam, and I heard that he was placed under the care of a psychiatrist, and re- covered the use of his eyes in a month or so. I suppose he was so fearful of failing that he couldn't face the ordeal of taking the test, and his unconscious helped him out by offering him a most effec- tive excuse.

PSYCHOANALYST: That's a more than usually clear case. Most symptoms of hysterics aren't that obvious. Sometimes there is only a lessening or distortion of sensation; or some sleepwalking epi- sodes; often a person divorces the emotional significance from a disturbing event so that, for instance, a young woman appears to be completely unmoved by the death of her father, and brings down on her head a good deal of unwarranted criticism for her callousness. One of Freud's most famous cases—it was recently dramatized in *A Far Country*—was that of an hysterical conversion. A young lady whom Freud called Fraülein Elisabeth found her legs paralyzed immediately after the death of her sister, and she didn't recover until Freud helped her, through analysis, to face without guilt the fact that she had fallen in love with her sister's husband. As she had stood at the bedside of her dead sister, for a single moment the thought had flashed through her mind that now her brother-in-law was free and could marry her. This idea had been so repugnant to her that it and the ensuing guilt were buried at once, only to reappear disguised in the symptom of the crippled legs which couldn't run to her beloved.

CAREER GIRL: Is this a major form of neurosis? I'm sure I've never seen a case of it.

PSYCHOANALYST: Actually, there are far fewer cases of conversion hysteria today than when Freud was formulating his theories.

CAREER GIRL: Why is that?

PSYCHOANALYST: Probably because of the cultural climate. Conversion hysteria is frequently rooted in forbidden sexual desires, but people are much more sophisticated and permissive now, and there's far less authoritarianism and sexual prudery than in Freud's day. The significance of sexual trauma—which was what Freud thought was most important—is indicated, moreover, in the fact that this kind of neurosis is particularly common in rural areas, where very frequently the family's sleeping arrangements invite an early and shattering view of the sexual act by a child.

TEACHER: By coincidence, I've just come across a validation of that point of view. Our concern in school for uncovering the capabilities of underprivileged children led me to read Frank Riesman's *The Culturally Deprived Child*. And in it he points out that the deprived individual—certainly the education and the sleeping arrangements are far from ideal in his home—is more likely to have conversion hysteria, if he becomes a neurotic, whereas the middle-class individual is more likely to express his neuroses in the form of obsessions and depressions.

HOUSEWIFE: People often speak of some individual as hysterical, and they don't mean those who have dramatic things wrong with them like blindness or deafness. Is the term incorrectly used?

PSYCHOANALYST: No. I've been using the psychoanalytical definition, and you are referring simply to the other, more popular definition of hysterical, as meaning uncontrollably emotional.

TEACHER: I believe you said that a person suffering from conversion hysteria shows no actual organic change in the affected limbs or organs. Is such hysteria completely unrelated to psychosomatic illness then?

PSYCHOANALYST: By medical definition, yes. Psychosomatic conditions show real organic signs of illness, although they are at least partially caused by the emotions. A person with psychosomatic colitis doesn't imagine that his colon is sensitive and bleeding—it really *is;* a person with psychosomatic heart pains will actually show organic results—constricted blood vessels and muscle damage. But the body and mind don't recognize this strict medical separation. Today we are more and more aware of the influence of both conscious and unconscious mental forces on physical health. The capacity of the emotions to produce organic disease has been attested to not only in heart disease and ulcers, but in allergies and migraines, blood pressure, obesity, indigestion, and constipation. And that's not all. It's known to operate in rheumatism, various eye and ear troubles, arthritis, and tuberculosis—and probably a good many other illnesses.

LAWYER: I can understand it with headaches and hives, but there's no end to the trend. Every time I get sick, instead of asking me what I ate, my wife wants to know what happened in court.

PSYCHOANALYST: You really shouldn't be so surprised. Our clichés show that people have been aware of the facts for years. Look at the sayings, "I've got butterflies in my stomach" and "Don't get your blood pressure up" and "Don't get your bowels in an uproar."

CAREER GIRL: Yes, and how about "to swallow your pride," or "to get a load off your chest," or "to die of a broken heart."

LAWYER: Well, your mind may make the trouble, but you still need plain old medicine to remove it.

PSYCHOANALYST: Would that it were that simple! I wouldn't suggest that we give up the treatment of organic disease by physical means, but some of these illnesses, like the allergies and ulcers, are particularly resistant to physical therapies, and particularly responsive to psychoanalysis; in fact, it can cure many a case which yields to nothing else.

TEACHER: Let's see—you've mentioned, as major neuroses, the phobias, obsessive-compulsive states, and hysterical conversion—almost all of which, you say, involve some accompanying anxiety. Is anxiety, then, just a part of every neurosis? I'm sure I've heard of an anxiety neurosis. Is that a special kind? Or do I have two things confused?

PSYCHOANALYST: No, you're quite right. There is a neurosis in which the outstanding symptom is anxiety without any conscious motivation, so that patients have difficulty in describing it precisely. Sometimes it's a fear of some vague impending catastrophe, or just of behaving foolishly. One patient feels anxious in the presence of particular persons, while another one feels anxious only when he's alone.

HOUSEWIFE: Is there a specific cause?

PSYCHOANALYST: It's the same cause that produces anxiety in other neuroses. When some event threatens to uncover a repressed impulse, there will be a feeling of anxiety as a reaction. Remember *Tea and Sympathy?* The young man was able to disregard the feminine aspects of his personality and lead a normal life until his masculinity was challenged. Then, faced with the need to prove himself a man with the campus whore, he became so anxious that he found himself impotent.

An anxiety state is often only the first phase of another neurosis. It rarely lasts in its purest form, although it does tend to recur periodically. When the illness develops, however, it assumes different forms in its later course, depending on the type of defense the personality puts up. If repressed anger is turned against one's self, depression develops; if it emerges as a disconnected idea, an obsessional neurosis may be formed, such as a fanatical hatred of Jews or Negroes, or a persecution complex. Free-floating anxiety may be the prelude to almost any form of neurosis or psychosis, since all these mental illnesses develop in an attempt to eliminate anxiety. An anxiety neurosis, then, is a state in which the personality has not yet succeeded in defending itself against the anxiety.

LAWYER: You mentioned depression. Is that a neurosis in itself?

PSYCHOANALYST: Sometimes. A neurotic depression may be an irrational response to a loss, one that can't be overcome by one's own efforts. There may be a feeling of hopelessness, embitterment, and a general lack of initiative, and the capacity for working may be affected, but a patient in such a depression is still able to maintain relations with others. It is not so severe as melancholia or psychotic depression.

TEACHER: You said, I think, that pathological depressions occur when the feelings of hostility a person has are turned against himself.

PSYCHOANALYST: Yes.

TEACHER: But does this mean that there is hostility involved in the depression of extreme grief? Why should there be hostility involved when you lose someone you love? One of our faculty members was a man who loved his wife very deeply, and when she died, he became so depressed he had to leave work for months. Were there, then, hostile feelings toward his dead wife?

PSYCHOANALYST: I would say it was very likely that there *were*, but that he was unaware of them. This man may have been angry at his wife for deserting him—in death—when he loved and wanted her. But of course such anger is not acceptable, either to the world or to his conscious mind, so it would be turned inward. Such a severe and prolonged reaction to a death does seem pathological, although of course I can't be sure that the explanation I've suggested for your colleague's depression is correct.

Hostility may be more deeply rooted. I had a woman as a patient, for example, who had led a very hard life, having had to work long hours to support a chronically ill son. She managed very well, however, until her luck changed. She inherited a good deal of money, and about the same time a new drug came along which brought immense improvement to her son's health. But the good luck, strangely enough, brought on a depression which grew steadily worse, until finally she undertook analysis. We discovered that she had developed heavy feelings of guilt as a result of her repressed hatred for her thoughtlessly cruel mother. As long as she had led her miserable life, she felt sufficiently punished for these feelings, but as soon as her circumstances improved through good luck and her life became enjoyable, the guilt overwhelmed her.

CAREER GIRL: Oh, the poor thing. I don't care for that symptom at all. Have you anything else to offer?

PSYCHOANALYST: There are a great many other neurotic symptoms, often related, as I said before. Inhibitions, including impotency and stammering, are frequently seen in connection with other symptoms. Unjustified fatigue, general feelings of inadequacy, moments of panic or suspicion or jealousy, and an inability to adjust or forgive are others.

TEACHER: You haven't mentioned hypochondria. Isn't that considered a neurosis? One of the painting teachers at school is always fretting over possible bruises to her fingers and complaining about pains in her arm, and the rest of us have always considered her neurotic.

PSYCHOANALYST: Yes, I dare say she's neurotic, although it would be safer to say so only after she'd had a thorough physical examination. Hypochondria is a neurosis, although generally it's tied in with other neurotic or psychotic symptoms—particularly with depressions and schizophrenias. The hypochondriac is persistently and irrationally overconcerned with his state of health. He often has symptoms of anxiety or depression, occasionally he has actual bodily sensations, and sometimes he has a fearful expectation of death. We sometimes see such symptoms in once beautiful, very self-centered women who can't reconcile themselves to growing old. They give their bodies the love and attention they had once received from their admirers.

LAWYER: You've certainly described a bunch of pitiful people. I'd hate to have any of them on any jury of mine.

PSYCHOANALYST: Yes; I'm afraid you can't expect a neurotic person to react in the rational fashion of an ideal juror. He's like a typewriter with a broken key. The work which the typewriter produces is fine if you don't hit that key. But whenever you do, the defect shows and distortion results. That's why neurotics are known by their inability to respond suitably, or in ways which are beneficial to them. That's why, indeed, they seem to do things that harm them even though they are intelligent, sane people.

CAREER GIRL: Is that really possible? How can it be?

PSYCHOANALYST: The anxiety of a neurotic is so intense that any behavior which brings immediate relief, even at the expense of long-term needs, is adopted. You might think, for instance, that the compulsive talker, who has experienced the throes of remorse for having sounded like an idiot and a fool, and who has watched the look of boredom creep over the faces of her listeners, would keep quiet. But that feeling of anxiety which is eased by her chatter is so painful if she does nothing about it that no conscious decision on her part can silence her. Once she finds the pain reduced by her compulsive action she naturally tends to repeat it. Thus such neurotic behavior becomes ingrained.

HOUSEWIFE: But then how can neurotics be helped?

PSYCHOANALYST: They can't, as a matter of fact, unless the pain —that is, the anxiety itself—is so severe that their neurotic acts no longer satisfy them, or unless they are so disabled by the neurosis as to recognize the need for help. Neurotics *do* have a large area in which the conscious processes operate, and this enables them to see how tragic and wasteful their actions are. But the fact is that if their acts satisfy them, it makes little difference to them if the rest of society, including their family, is harmed by them. A large proportion of homosexuals, for instance, have no basic urge to give up their behavior; they are very resistant to therapeutic change because they receive too much satisfaction from their sex patterns. And there are, similarly, a number of other kinds of behavior, sometimes grouped under the heading of personality or character disorders, which are very difficult to treat, since the people who so behave are not easily aroused to anxiety by their acts. Broadly speaking, most sexual deviants, the addicts, and psychopaths or antisocial characters can be considered to belong in this category.

HOUSEWIFE: What kinds of sexual deviants do you mean?

PSYCHOANALYST: People given to compulsive promiscuity, for one example. Then the people who enjoy sexual perversions of one kind or other; the men who like little boys or girls—I'm sure you remember *Lolita;* the ones who receive sexual satisfaction from an object of clothing rather than a person—

TEACHER: That's fetishism, isn't it?

PSYCHOANALYST: Yes. Then there's exhibitionism, or exposing oneself before another person; voyeurism, or watching another person who's nude; masturbation; transvestism—

LAWYER: That's when men put on women's clothing, isn't it? Or vice versa? You mean that's a real sexual kick in itself? I thought it was just to show the other boys what they were.

PSYCHOANALYST: It seems to provide a thrill in itself to those who do it. Then there are the people who get their enjoyment from animals, either by watching them copulate or by having intercourse with the animals themselves.

TEACHER: Aren't sadism and masochism considered perversions, too?

PSYCHOANALYST: Right. The conscious sexual satisfaction received from inflicting pain (which is what we mean by sadism), or the sexual enjoyment received from suffering (which is what we mean by masochism) are indeed perversions. And although we read in the papers about the more horrible examples—men who tear off or mutilate the breasts of women—there are a great many lesser kinds, such as those who need to beat or be beaten with straps until seeing the welts brings an orgasm, from which both parties derive such satisfaction that neither ever seeks treatment.

HOUSEWIFE: That seems incredible.

PSYCHOANALYST: "There are more things in heaven and earth, Horatio, than are dreamt of in your philosophy."

LAWYER: And how about the lust murderers?

PSYCHOANALYST: Yes, the ones who kill in order to have sexual intercourse with a corpse. Sick people, all.

HOUSEWIFE: And they can't be helped?

PYCHOANALYST: I didn't say that. I said it was very difficult. But analysis is still the best available means of cure, and new techniques are being developed all the time. And if such people come to analysis for the treatment of some other neurotic symptom, they can frequently be given enough insight into their unconscious motives to encourage them to continue until they can have normal sexual relationships.

LAWYER: You said that addicts, too, are difficult to help because they don't feel uncomfortable enough about their difficulties. I don't know about the young punks who take dope, but surely that doesn't apply to alcoholics. Why, I've known some fine people—even a judge, as a matter of fact—who've become alcoholics, and after a bender they're just smothered in remorse.

PSYCHOANALYST: But the very reason they *are* alcoholics and drug addicts is that they can find release from underlying conflicts and anxieties in their addiction. What these people have in common is an inability to stand frustration and disappointment, a feeling of inferiority, and an overwhelming need to get rid of their hostility and guilt. That's why, except for long-time members of A.A., the analytic treatment of addicts is best carried out in the confined conditions of a sanitarium, where it is impossible for them to receive the solace of drink or drugs. It's obvious what a tremendous problem this poses, considering the limited number of analysts and hospitals and the length of time treatment requires.

TEACHER: Do I understand you correctly? Is it a lack in their character that makes them unable to bear the anxiety and so turn to drugs or alcohol, rather than the addiction that ruins their character?

PSYCHOANALYST: "Character" is a very broad word. I would prefer to say that they all suffer to some extent from a disorder of the personality, which makes them incapable of mature behavior. This disorder is more clearly developed, and better known, in what most psychiatrists refer to as the psychopathic personality.

HOUSEWIFE: I thought a psychopath was anybody who acted in a crazy—pardon me, irrational—manner.

PSYCHOANALYST: Popularly, the term is often used in that fashion, but professionally it refers specifically to the chronically antisocial, impulsive person who is always in trouble; who learns nothing from experience or advice, from rewards or punishment —including jail; who has no loyalties to any person—mother, wife, or child—or to any group or moral code. He is emotionally a selfish child, who wants what he wants when he wants it. He has no sense of responsibility or judgment. He can make anything he desires sound perfectly reasonable by his capacity for rationalization.

TEACHER: Is such a person immature because of low intelligence?

PSYCHOANALYST: Not at all. Frequently he has unusual ability and intelligence. He is fully aware of the social amenities and of the accepted social code. He seems so rational and aware of the wrongs he has committed that he is almost always considered legally sane. But he has no conscience. He will steal, forge checks, commit bigamy, go to bed easily with any number of women—and not infrequently with men—desert his family, and even murder upon little or no provocation. The majority of psychopaths, however, seem to avoid crimes grave enough to send them to jail for long terms. But when such types do become criminals, they are the most dangerous kind, because they feel no compunction. They seem to suffer from no anxiety, such as ordinary neurotics have, nor do they indulge in the obvious irrational behavior and thinking of psychotics.

LAWYER: They sound like plain criminals to me. I've come across scores of such people in my practice.

PSYCHOANALYST: You probably have. But most habitual criminals, although they show some features of the psychopath, work more consistently toward their own goals, have loyalties of their own, and spend their ill-deserved gains in a more sensible fashion. The real psychopath cares about nothing. Here's a case to illustrate: a boy I know of had never shown any interest in school, and the truant officers were often after him. Yet he didn't stay away from school because he had anything else in particular that he wanted to do. Instead, he wandered about indulging in acts of petty mischief, such as setting fire to an old shed, or removing somebody's gate and tossing it into the stream. Sometimes he stole things from his parents—a ring or a silver pitcher—but he wasn't really interested in them or in what the money could buy, and sold them for practically nothing or traded them for some other momentarily desirable object. Each time he was found out—and he always was—he seemed contrite and aware of what he had done, and seriously promised never to do such things again. But he always reneged on the promise. By the time he was in his late teens he was taking the cars which belonged to his neighbors and even to strangers and just going for a ride in them. He was arrested again and again—he had had over seventy arrests by the time he was in his early twenties—but the imprisonments meant nothing to him. His family constantly tried to smooth things over for him, because he was so logical and so seemingly sincere about turning over a new leaf. Such a person would be most difficult to treat. As I said, he feels no anxiety, sees no need for treatment. If the analyst can succeed in arousing enough anxiety, he may be able to hold on to him, but usually such a patient leaves almost as soon as he begins.

TEACHER: Is such an individual considered neurotic? With

the same mixture of environmental and hereditary elements causing his behavior?

PSYCHOANALYST: There is a good deal of speculation on the subject, and many people prefer to classify psychopaths separately from neurotics. Too, because these antisocial people are so difficult to treat by regular psychotherapeutic methods, there is a tendency to look for a greater congenital factor. But no isolated cause—at least, not yet—has been found to explain them.

HOUSEWIFE: And nothing can be done about them?

PSYCHOANALYST: We certainly don't have any sure treatment yet. But these people don't want to go to jail, so there's *some* motivation to work with; that's why judges are sometimes able to sentence them, but parole them on the condition that they enter therapy. In short, we're groping for a method, a combination of therapeutic and legal means, to keep such people from inflicting harm on society. After all, we recognize the need for such methods in dealing with psychotics, so why not with psychopaths?

HOUSEWIFE: Oh, yes, the psychotics. You haven't told us about them yet.

PSYCHOANALYST: I did say, you recall, that in the psychotic the unconscious processes quite overwhelm the conscious ones. This defeat is expressed by behavior which disregards the objective world. Psychotics are so clearly helpless that society recognizes and tolerates them, and seeks only to protect itself by quarantining them. The man who withdraws so completely into depression that he won't even eat, the woman who hits a man over the head with a bottle because a voice told her to, the student who is found hanging from a rafter in his room—these are all psychotics. They may not be constantly out of touch with the world; perhaps they will only have episodes of disorganization. But they need treatment and protection.

TEACHER: What causes this victory of the unconscious in psychosis?

PSYCHOANALYST: Well, in organic psychosis the cause is physical. It might be a brain injury or a tumor, congenital mental retardation or a glandular disease, or the deterioration of old age. It might be the result of certain poisons, or alcohol, or syphilis. But we are more concerned here with functional psychosis, which is found in cases whose brains are apparently normal.

HOUSEWIFE: What causes functional psychosis then?

PSYCHOANALYST: Perhaps it's simply a more intense form of neurosis, in which the increase in intensity produces something quite different—an abrupt collapse of the personality's defenses. Or perhaps it is a distinctly different kind of psychological disorder from neurosis; certainly psychosis often comes over a patient abruptly—and leaves rather abruptly—whereas neurosis can last a lifetime. But we don't really know why a particular person becomes psychotic rather than neurotic, whether it's a stronger hereditary predisposition or greater stress or some combination of both of these. A recent survey, conducted by a sociologist of the Cornell Medical College's Department of Psychiatry, indicated, for instance, that when people are faced with great pressures, those of lower economic and social status tend to react psychotically, while those of higher status tend to react neurotically. But this only raises more questions. I'm afraid I can't give you a clear-cut answer.

HOUSEWIFE: Are there many different kinds of psychosis?

PSYCHOANALYST: There are several general classifications of functional psychoses. The one most familiar in literature, but a minor problem today, is the manic-depressive, whose swings of mood are exaggerated from one extreme to the other and who is overwhelmed by both states.

TEACHER: What are the symptoms?

PSYCHOANALYST: In the manic phase, or mania, the patient is restless and agitated, frequently becomes sexually uninhibited, talks volubly and excitedly, and laughs a great deal. In fact, he may be almost indistinguishable from the happy drunk, although he's even less rational, of course, and if crossed he can become irritable and violent. This condition may continue for days or weeks or months.

TEACHER: And what happens in the depressive stage?

PSYCHOANALYST: Suddenly the machine falters; the patient finds each thought and act slow, hard work; he has no initiative, no self-confidence, no interest in sex; he becomes preoccupied with somber thoughts and finally settles into a deep depression. Sometimes he even becomes suicidal.

CAREER GIRL: Do these two phases always go together in the same person?

PSYCHOANALYST: Yes, they do, although there are other psychotic depressions. A major one, in fact, is involutional psychosis—the reaction to the change of life, the biologically and socially regressive stage which overtakes a good many women and not a few men. It usually involves extreme gloom, and sometimes feelings of guilt, anxiety, agitation, preoccupation with real or imagined bodily ills, and other delusional ideas. This used to be a much more serious disorder, but the new drugs and electric shock treatments are very effective against it.

TEACHER: How about the manic-depressive state? Is that serious?

PSYCHOANALYST: Well, people do tend to recover from it, but they also can have recurrences. Of course, here, too, the new treatments are highly effective.

TEACHER: What other kinds of psychosis are there?

PSYCHOANALYST: The major group, far greater in severity and number of cases than any other kind, is the schizophrenias. These were once known by the name of dementia praecox, or premature insanity, because the disease is very apt to begin during puberty. In fact, according to Dr. A. A. Brill, probably 75 percent of schizophrenic attacks occur between the ages of fourteen and eighteen, and 90 percent between the ages of fifteen and twenty-five, with the others coming later.

TEACHER: Why do you use the plural term—schizophrenias?

PSYCHOANALYST: Because they have so many different symptoms. Perhaps more experience will show that there are really a number of separate diseases. In simple schizophrenic reactions, the individual withdraws from the struggle of life, becomes disinterested and emotionally apathetic, and shows a slow but gradual personality disintegration. When this withdrawal reaches its ultimate degree, the regression, ridiculous actions, and gibberish appear. Because all this often happens gradually, the illness may be quite well developed before other people are aware of it. For example, a mother brought her fifteen-year-old daughter to me for treatment. She told me that the girl had been perfectly well up to about five months earlier, at which time she began to sit around the house listlessly, didn't want to be bothered dressing, and took no interest in her schoolwork. When I went into the matter, I found that there had been signs of the disease long before then, but her parents had thought the girl merely lazy.

HOUSEWIFE: Yes, I guess that's what I would have thought.

PSYCHOANALYST: It is true that the average parent doesn't realize the gravity of a situation until the school, perhaps, sends home a report that the child is failing and doesn't seem to care at all. But it is a sure sign that there is danger ahead when a girl who has been apparently well suddenly becomes indifferent to the things that interest the average young woman of her age— attractive clothes, good marks, girl friends, and dates with boys.

HOUSEWIFE: But all schizophrenics don't act the same way, you said. How else might they behave?

PSYCHOANALYST: There are a number of possibilities. One is the catatonic reaction, which I'm sure you've seen in the movies. The patient exhibits an immobility and rigidity of a part or all of his body. Lift his arm and he will be unable to lower it; talk to him and he will be incapable of answering you. There are also the schizophrenics with hallucinations. They may hear voices or see visions. Sometimes these people are dangerous. Their unconscious aggressiveness may find a vent in the imagined voice that tells them to kill.

TEACHER: Are there many schizophrenics who are dangerous?

PSYCHOANALYST: No, there aren't. Indeed, the proportion of all mental hospital patients who are wild and out of control is about the same as the proportion of airplane crashes to safe flights. Even when schizophrenics talk of dangers and enemies, it's more likely that they will be like one pathetic woman I saw in a mental hospital. She didn't hallucinate, but she had delusions that she was a victim of the Communists. They had her put in the hospital, she said, because she had been trying to protect Henry Morgan, the humorist, from them. She had met him, as she told the story, during common work, and an affair of the heart had been the result. But the Communists had coerced Mr. Morgan into marrying the head of their gang, and had gotten her fired and sent to the mental institution.

HOUSEWIFE: Was any of it true?

PSYCHOANALYST: No, she had never even met Henry Morgan. But she had never bothered him either, and was completely harmless; as a matter of fact, the director of the hospital was preparing to release her at the time I was last there.

CAREER GIRL: She sounds paranoid to me.

PSYCHOANALYST: That's true. She was a paranoid schizophrenic.

LAWYER: What does that mean?

CAREER GIRL: She had delusions of persecution.

HOUSEWIFE: I've always been confused about that word "paranoid." Is it used to describe anyone who thinks someone's after him—like the fellow who's sure he's a failure because the Catholics keep people from patronizing his business—or only for people who have to be sent to a mental hospital?

PSYCHOANALYST: It's no wonder you're confused. Paranoid characteristics can be found in people who have no other schizophrenic signs; that is, their contacts with reality are normal, they don't hallucinate, they aren't withdrawn or depressed. Such people are not considered schizophrenic. But then even the paranoid schizophrenic is less likely than other schizophrenics to lose complete contact with reality, so with each case there is a particularly difficult diagnostic decision to be made. And, naturally, no layman can make it.

LAWYER: We get your message, Doctor. Well, once the decision has been made, and you find you have a schizophrenic, can you cure him?

PSYCHOANALYST: First of all, we don't like to use the word "cure." What psychiatry tries to do is to restore the control of conscious forces. If the schizophrenic, or any psychotic for that matter, is so out of contact with reality that he can't be reached with psychotherapy, the institution must offer him what help it can. And there is a great deal of it today—drugs, occupational therapy, work therapy, protective surroundings. Whenever possible, between psychotic episodes, for instance, psychotherapy or analysis can be useful. With all the means of treatment available today, the chances for partial or total recovery from schizophrenia have jumped from 20 to 70 percent in the last forty years.

CAREER GIRL: That's dramatic enough. I could really build an advertising campaign around comparative figures like that.

TEACHER: You seem to feel, then, that psychoanalysis is useful in almost all mental disturbances?

PSYCHOANALYST: Let me recapitulate. Although psychoanalysis cannot be used to shield the patient from the accidents of life, or prevent primarily organic diseases, it can increase the patient's resistances to adversity and disease by lessening the destructive influence of unconscious forces, and its influence is most significant where these unconscious forces are most important. It cannot, however, treat all illnesses with the same degree of effectiveness. After all, no one expects surgery to achieve the same results in cancer as in appendicitis. The neuroses are particularly amenable to analytic treatment, and it has had a much more limited, but increasing, success with the psychoses, the character disorders, and the psychosomatic illnesses.

TEACHER: You suggest analysis, then, for everyone with a neurosis? An analyst never turns anyone down?

PSYCHOANALYST: Yes, he does, since his acceptance of a case implies his belief that the patient will benefit from the treatment.

CAREER GIRL: Well, don't you feel that every neurotic person *can* benefit?

PSYCHOANALYST: Unfortunately, no. There are criteria which a patient must meet.

LAWYER: What are they?

PSYCHOANALYST: First of all, he must want to get better enough to put aside the feeling of shame and guilt which society still attaches to mental illness. Next, he must be hurting. He might not be, you know. This is why the character disorders are so difficult to treat, as I indicated earlier. Sometimes it's chiefly the family and friends who suffer. One of the special peculiarities of the neurotic process is that some people can turn their neurotic weaknesses into self-gratifying or socially acceptable activities. The man who's afraid to compete but convinces himself he's a philosopher, an onlooker of life, is quite smug about not taking part in the all-too-necessary struggle for existence. The martyr brings misery to his immediate family, but he finds his sacrifices deeply rewarding. And the man whose neurosis compels him to drive himself to success after success cares nothing about the people he's harmed on the way up. Such people are unlikely to come to analysis at all, and if they do, it is usually as the result of prodding by others. When this is what brings them, they are unlikely to stick it out, and the analyst is well aware of this at the outset.

HOUSEWIFE: Maybe if the mistreated family wouldn't put up with the neurotic's actions it would be a good thing.

PSYCHOANALYST: It would, indeed. It's ironic that tender and loving patience, if misapplied, can actually block the road to health. Every person must pay the price for his neurosis. If the family takes over the debt, he himself will suffer little pain, and feel no need for treatment.

CAREER GIRL: It seems to me that many neurotic people feel they're special and cherish their little neuroses.

PSYCHOANALYST: You're right. Frequently a patient feels that all that keeps him from being a nonentity is his illness. He's afraid that if he were stripped of his neurotic eccentricity, he would lose all individuality and creativeness.

LAWYER: And this isn't true?

PSYCHOANALYST: Actually, once he's freed of his neurotic insecurity, he becomes more productive and less timid and conformist than before.

LAWYER: Then you can't treat a patient unless he really wants you to?

PSYCHOANALYST: With some exceptions, that's true. The most important exception is the adolescent, who, though he is resentful, resistant, and uncomprehending, will need the substitute parent, which the analyst represents, enough to stay with him.

TEACHER: How about even younger children? Are there any restrictions as to age?

PSYCHOANALYST: Yes, there are. Because of the very nature of psychotherapy, the child must be able to talk, to make himself understood verbally, before treatment can conceivably be begun. And then, of course, there is no question of his understanding the process or lying on a couch. Special methods must be used for young children. But the young are healed so much more readily than the old! The neurotic stamp on a person's behavior becomes more deeply imprinted with every accommodating action, until it is sometimes impossible to remove.

TEACHER: How about intelligence? Does it matter that a patient is not bright or well educated?

PSYCHOANALYST: Formal education matters very little, but

there's no question that intelligence is an asset. Again, there's no exact line which can be drawn.

TEACHER: Then your ideal patient is someone with a neurosis which hurts him, which he is willing to lose, which hasn't become hopelessly ingrained from long years of patronage, and which is accompanied by enough of a mind to understand what's going on in it.

PSYCHOANALYST: Yes. But that's not to say that analysts don't often take patients who are not ideal. Analysis is so young a technique that it would be deadening and wasteful to refuse less than ideal cases. As I said before, analysis is also a method of investigation, of acquiring knowledge about the mind.

LAWYER: With human guinea pigs!

PSYCHOANALYST: I'm afraid that psychoanalysis is only practicable with human beings. But even when it doesn't effect a recovery, it usually brings about some improvement—and at least it doesn't kill, as some earlier medical practices not infrequently did. And surely you'll admit that our efforts have been justified not only by our successes but also by all that we've learned—and just discussed—about the mental patient and his illnesses.

CHAPTER FOUR

OEDIPUS AND ALL THAT

*A thumbnail history of psychoanalysis: some of Freud's major
theoretical discoveries, including the unconscious, the nature
of repressions, infantile sexuality, the Oedipus complex, the
instinctual drives, the ego, id and superego; Freud's disciples
and dissenters; present influences in the field.*

PSYCHOANALYST: At long last I've come to the point where I'm
ready to tell you about Freud's discoveries. And I never cease to
be stirred by the realization that one man, by his genius, was able
to affect the lives of so many people in the Western world. More
than that, the discoveries are such that they seem always to have
been known. And yet, perhaps only Galileo and Darwin caused a
furor of comparable intensity by simply drawing conclusions from
facts which were available to everyone. It's understandable, I
suppose. If people felt their position in the universe was im-
periled by these two earlier men, how much more were they
alarmed by Freud, whose theories threatened the autonomy of
their very minds.

HOUSEWIFE: I'm a little ashamed to admit it, but I'm very
hazy about Freud's theories, and his life, too, for that matter. I
think of him rather vaguely as the Father of Psychoanalysis, but
I don't suppose the idea sprang full-blown from his forehead like
Athena from Zeus.

PSYCHOANALYST: Great ideas rarely come about like that, do
they? Certainly this one didn't. Sigmund Freud was a doctor, and
it was through his practice that he discovered the great truths
which he made known to the world, but without a great deal of
knowledge he slowly acquired from his contemporaries as well as

from literature he couldn't have made the discoveries. He himself would have been the first to say so.

HOUSEWIFE: He wasn't a regular doctor, was he?

PSYCHOANALYST: He didn't have a general practice, if that's what you mean, but he was a physician. While he was still a medical student, he felt that psychiatry—such as it was in the 1880's—was particularly challenging, and so he concentrated on nervous diseases.

TEACHER: Was he living in Vienna then?

PSYCHOANALYST: Yes, he lived most of his life in Vienna. But in 1885 he went to study in Paris under Jean Martin Charcot, a physician who was becoming famous for his use of hypnotism in the treatment of hysteria—by which I mean *conversion hysteria,* of which we spoke earlier. Charcot would first hypnotize his patients, then suggest that when they awoke they would no longer have their symptoms, and by so doing he was able to bring temporary relief to many people who were paralyzed, or had palsy-like tremor or other hysterical manifestations. The year Freud spent with the French physician convinced him of the usefulness of hypnosis, and he came back to Vienna and in his own practice tried to use what he had learned. This was a time when nervous ailments were treated by physical means, which consisted of little more than a sedative for an excited patient and a tonic for a depressed one. Thoughtful physicians recognized how ineffectual such treatments were for nervous disorders, but they knew of nothing else to do.

LAWYER: Did Freud succeed with hypnotism?

PSYCHOANALYST: He used it a good deal during the first few years of his private practice, but rapidly discovered that not all patients could be hypnotized, and even when they were, and responded to posthypnotic suggestion, they didn't remain cured. In the meantime, however, he had learned of an unusual case from Dr. Josef Breuer, a prominent and considerably older physician who had also been working with cases of hysteria by hypnosis. And in this case there was something new that eventually led him beyond the superficial effects of hypnosis.

CAREER GIRL: Ah, this must be the famous case of Anna O.

PSYCHOANALYST: Famous, and justly so. Breuer had been called in to treat a young woman who had become ill while nursing her father, to whom she was very deeply attached. She developed a variety of symptoms: at first there was a nervous cough; then she refused to eat and lost weight; next came severe headaches; finally, both legs and her right arm felt paralyzed. Breuer had helped her considerably by hypnotic suggestion, and got many of her symptoms to disappear, but then her father died, and she collapsed, all her former symptoms returning in full force. Again Breuer hypnotized her and suddenly, while under hypnosis one day, and with no prompting from him, she began to speak excitedly and with deep emotion of events which involved her father. This happened repeatedly thereafter, during her treatment time. And as the months went on, and as Anna, under hypnosis, would talk about all the things which were troubling her so, the symptoms which seemed to be connected with each event disappeared.

LAWYER: She did all this under hypnosis? She wasn't aware of what she was doing?

PSYCHOANALYST: When she was awake, Anna knew nothing about the origin of her symptoms, but in a hypnotic trance she immediately knew the connection and could talk about it. For instance, she had started to cough for the first time while sitting by her father's bed and hearing dance music from a neighbor's house. She wanted to go to the dance, thought of asking permission, and promptly felt guilty at the desire—and began to cough. Throughout her illness she reacted to music by coughing, as though still inhibiting her original desire. In the same way, as she talked about the past it appeared that each of her symptoms had come into being in situations where an impulse to do something had to be forbidden by her conscience.

TEACHER: Then it was Breuer, and not Freud, who first discovered the unconscious and repressions.

PSYCHOANALYST: No—Breuer didn't recognize the significance of what had happened. He did know that he had discovered a useful way to treat patients whose hysteria was due to repressed material, but even Freud, when he heard of the case, didn't realize the complete nature and full extent of either repressions or the unconscious. However, Breuer was certainly the first to use "the talking cure," as Anna O. called it, and Freud recognized its value. Freud then tested this method himself for several years and found ample proof of its validity. Then, on Freud's urging, the two men published, first, a preliminary paper, and then, in 1895, a book, *Studies in Hysteria,* which contained descriptions of the cases of Anna O. and a number of their other patients. In this publication they explained what they called the "cathartic method," concluding that its efficacy rested on the mental and emotional purging which the patient went through during the treatment. They suggested, too, that hysterical symptoms were the result of some disagreeable and forgotten—that is, repressed—episode from the patient's life, although the patient himself neither understood the significance of nor could consciously control the symptoms.

TEACHER: Why do we hear so little of Breuer?

PSYCHOANALYST: Because very soon after their joint publication, which didn't touch on the *origin* of repressions, Breuer became frightened by Freud's exploration into the causes of neuroses. Breuer had established a lucrative practice and had a high reputation as a family physician; and Freud's growing belief in the sexual nature of the illnesses they were treating seemed likely to cost Breuer his security. You can imagine the storm which bade fair to be aroused by such disclosures in that prudish, inhibited era. So Breuer withdrew, and Freud went on alone. At no little cost to his practice, I might add; Breuer was right to fear the opposition.

CAREER GIRL: But what happened to hypnotism? I know Freud didn't always use it.

PSYCHOANALYST: Freud abandoned hypnosis gradually, during this same period—the early 1890's. You recall that I said he wasn't able to induce hypnosis in all his patients, in spite of studying with Charcot in Paris and with other French hypnotists at Nancy. But he recalled one incident which had occurred when he was watching Dr. Hyppolyte Bernheim at Nancy in 1889. Bernheim had hypnotized a patient, and later, after awakening her, was able without posthypnotic suggestions, but only by urging, to get her to recall everything she had done under hypnosis. Freud reasoned that if a patient could remember what she had forgotten under hypnosis, she ought to be able to remember what she had forgotten hysterically as well. Acting on this belief, he urged his patients simply to talk to him. And from the long hesitancies and silences of one of his patients, Fräulein Elisabeth, he recognized that she was holding back pertinent information; and so he gradually developed his method of working into one in which the patient said anything at all which came to mind, no matter how unimportant or disgraceful it seemed.

TEACHER: That's known as free association, isn't it?

PSYCHOANALYST: Yes, and enormously important it is, too, but I would rather discuss the technique itself more fully some other time. Just let me say now that through this method Freud was able to prove that in the mind, as in all of nature, nothing happens without cause. Each psychic event is determined by the ones which precede it. Even when such events appear completely accidental, they are not really so. But his tremendous discovery was that the unconscious plays an enormous part in our mental processes. Errors, slips of tongue or pen, lapses of memory, all have their causes in the workings of the unconscious and are traceable to that source.

LAWYER: I admit that some slips are clear enough. My wife never remembers to pay bills, for instance. And of course when you're tired you make mistakes, too. But can it really be proven beyond reasonable doubt that every single mistake is purposeful?

PSYCHOANALYST: It can, indeed; Freud did just that, in the *Psychopathology of Everyday Life,* which was published in 1904. Incidentally, being tired is not a reason for a slip—it just weakens your defenses so that your unconscious feelings have a better chance of coming through. The same thing happens when you're drinking.

LAWYER: But when I introduce someone I know well and suddenly forget his name, what could be the reason for that? It just doesn't make sense.

PSYCHOANALYST: I don't know *your* reasons, of course. They would undoubtedly be different for each forgotten name. Freud tells of addressing one of his patients as Mrs. Smith, when her name was really Mrs. James. When his attention was called to the mistake, he soon realized that he had another patient named James who refused to pay her bills, while still another patient named Smith paid promptly. Evidently, he wished Mrs. James would do so, too. But the discovery of the reason for a lapse of memory or a slip of the tongue is not always readily apparent.

One analyst told Freud of a patient who couldn't recall the name of the psychiatrist, Jung, which means "young," as you probably know. In trying to find the forgotten name, the patient thought of, among other things, a woman who seemed not to age and Oscar Wilde, whom she connected with homosexual relations with young men. It turned out that she was a widow at thirty-nine with no prospect of marrying a second time, and thoughts of her lost youth were painful to her. So you see, the connections with the unconscious may not be obvious at once, but they are there and can be found.

HOUSEWIFE: Then a Freudian slip isn't necessarily one with sexual significance.

PSYCHOANALYST: No, every slip is Freudian in the sense that Freud believed it to have an unconscious meaning. But though he didn't think all unconscious processes stemmed from sexual forces, he *did* believe, especially early in the development of his theories, that the neuroses had sexual roots. And the evidence he gathered was certainly unwelcome to his colleagues—and to himself, for that matter. He wrote, in fact, that he had a personal disinclination to single out the sexual factor. But years of listening to his patients and helping them to recover made it inevitable that he recognize the sexual influence. Then, too, he verified his findings by his own self-analysis.

LAWYER: Self-analysis? He analyzed himself?

PSYCHOANALYST: Yes, he felt he could better understand the possible effects of the unconscious processes of the mind, and therefore be of more use to his patients, if he knew *himself* and the workings of *his* mind. He also had persistent problems of his own—not so dramatic as his patients', it is true—which he wanted to solve. And no one who hasn't been analyzed can realize what an amazing feat that self-analysis was, especially when the technique was scarcely developed.

CAREER GIRL: How on earth did he do it?

PSYCHOANALYST: He had to invent and discover methods as he went along. He used his own dreams, for one thing. His discovery of the meaningfulness and the unconscious motivations of dreams was just as enormous and original as his discovery of the sexual conflicts behind hysteria.

TEACHER: Didn't he write *The Interpretation of Dreams* around that time?

PSYCHOANALYST: Yes, that epochal work was written in 1898. It was during the years before and during his work on this book that he came to the gradual realization that all children have incest wishes toward their parents, and recognized what has ever since been known as infantile sexuality.

LAWYER: I can understand his patients' having sexual problems. We all know the unnatural attitude toward love the people of that period had. But how did he come to the radical conclusion that children are sexually in love with their parents?

PSYCHOANALYST: It wasn't easy for him; he was a man of his own time, and he was undoubtedly more surprised and reluctant than you or any of us to admit the sexual basis of emotional illness, and even more reluctant to recognize the existence of infantile incestuous wishes. But it was his patients who gave him the raw data, and his own genius that saw the truth behind them. As he listened to his patients talking about their experiences, and tried to interpret their dreams, he heard a great many stories of childhood seduction by an adult, usually the parent; after a while, he could not avoid the conclusion that something deeply significant lay in this area. For a time he believed his patients' accounts of such seductions, and thought them to be the traumatic cause of the patients' illnesses; after a number of years, however, he realized that so many seductions couldn't have taken place, and, indeed, he found that some never had. So he revised his theory, and came to a far more important conclusion: namely, that these "recollections" represented the disguised and distorted *wishes* the patients had had as children. It was as if they had denied their own wishes and projected them onto the opposite-sex parent, saying, in effect, "I didn't want to do this, Daddy. But *you* did this to me."

HOUSEWIFE: Surely not every female patient believed she had been seduced by her father?

PSYCHOANALYST: Of course not. But there were other recollections, all filled with emotion, that added to Freud's conviction. Men's remembrances as little boys of seeing their mothers nude, women's memories of the intense pleasure the caresses of their fathers had given them when they were young, the repressed death wishes of patients of either sex toward parents of the opposite sex—all these had their part in convincing him. So it was that he came to believe that there were sexual experiences, or more commonly, feelings very much allied to sexual desire, early in childhood. He maintained that sex is born with the individual and that the energy of the sexual instinct—which he called the libido—is active from the very first.

LAWYER: I've heard that, too, and I must challenge that statement. *I* certainly don't recall those feelings as part of *my* childhood.

PSYCHOANALYST: It is precisely because of each person's own need to forget the sexual wishes and conflicts of his own early childhood that almost no one—at least before Freud's investigations—was able to recognize the presence of sexual wishes in children. But if you observe them, or talk with them objectively, it is certainly obvious. Just recall, for a moment, the flirtatious ways of a little girl toward her father, and the delight she takes in coming into his bed and snuggling up to him.

HOUSEWIFE: I certainly have seen children flirt.

PSYCHOANALYST: Of course, the recognition of the sexual drive in children was far from Freud's total contribution to our knowledge of the psychological forces influencing our behavior. Nor is the growth pattern he eventually described in *Three Contributions to the Theory of Sexuality* meant to be a diagram of the origin of neuroses. It is, however, a theory of normal character development which is widely accepted today.

As I summarize it for you, it may sound arbitrary, but you must understand that the stages are not distinct; they merge and overlap, so that the transition is gradual; and the duration of each stage is only approximate, too.

First comes the oral phase, which lasts for about the first year and a half. During this period the desires of the infant are based on the mouth, lips and tongue—organs that give strong gratifications, which, therefore, Freud considered to contain many of the elements of sexual pleasure.

LAWYER: I can see what pleasure the infant receives from sucking, but I don't understand why it should be called sexual.

PSYCHOANALYST: Freud believed that the libido—the sexual drive—was the basic cause of every effort to obtain pleasure. And there are many bits of evidence to support his theory—as, for instance, the existence of cases of abnormal sexual development in which infantile interests have become the chief source of adult sexual gratification. An individual who has developed in such a fashion might receive his only sexual satisfaction through the contact of his tongue and lips with another person's body; some sexual deviants are of this type.

TEACHER: I did read somewhere that even before Freud's theory was known a Hungarian pediatrician named Lindner had suggested that thumb-sucking was related to sexual pleasure.

PSYCHOANALYST: Yes. Lindner made the point that older children who indulged in this habit frequently masturbated at the same time. Freud felt that this article substantiated his own views. He pointed out that a characteristic of infantile sexuality is that a child can learn to satisfy its own needs if the object of its love is not available. That is, if the infant cannot always have its mother's breast, it soon learns to pacify itself by sucking its own fingers and toes.

HOUSEWIFE: Is that good or bad?

PSYCHOANALYST: Neither. It is simply a characteristic of that period of development. There are a number of ways a child can develop which many people believe show the influence of this phase, and many analysts, particularly Karl Abraham, one of Freud's earliest followers, have elaborated Freud's first proposals along these lines. Thumb-sucking gives a child a potential independence from the environment; it also leaves the way open for an excessive interest in himself. For some people, sucking—whether at the breast or the thumb—was so pleasant that as adults they remain optimistic and happy, enjoying food and drink enormously. Others who had harsh and abrupt weanings may show a striking hostility and dissatisfaction, or may even develop hysterical vomiting, for instance. In the normal course of development, however, the child is thought gradually to transfer his source of pleasure to the anus, as he reaches what is known as the anal phase.

TEACHER: But why should he discard the pleasures of sucking?

PSYCHOANALYST: It is more likely that *weaning removes* the pleasure. And it's probably because toilet training comes after weaning that the anal period seems to follow the oral phase.

Otherwise they would overlap much more obviously, as indeed they do in many primitive cultures. At any rate, this phase, too, lasts about a year and a half, and, as you can tell from the name, the anus is now the site of sexual tensions and pleasures. The baby enjoys not only defecating but withholding his feces.

HOUSEWIFE: Yes, to the despair of his mother!

LAWYER: Someone told me of the preposterous idea that because a child can't keep his feces he saves money instead, and that's why people like to be rich.

PSYCHOANALYST: I'm not going to deny that the social value of money is a powerful reason for a person's desiring it, but it has been observed that there is an emotional connection between money and excrement. That is, one's attitude toward money may be the adult *analogue* or *outgrowth* of his childish attitude toward excrement. This isn't surprising when you consider that his feces are the child's first possession, and that the mother offers inducements like praise or candy to persuade him to part with it.

CAREER GIRL: Hmm. A form of prewampum currency!

PSYCHOANALYST: It really is. In addition, there is the feeling of pride a child receives from the control of the act of defecation, accompanied as it is by the approval of his mother.

HOUSEWIFE: I guess it is a pretty important part of a child's life. It certainly took up a lot of *my* time and energy to toilet-train my son.

TEACHER: What effects on an adult's character is this anal period supposed to have, according to Freud and his friends?

PSYCHOANALYST: Their opinion was that those people who don't develop normally, but remain under the influence of this period are particularly orderly, obstinate, and parsimonious, frequently to the point of avarice. Almost all their relationships in life are proprietary. Sometimes, too, they are cruel and malicious.

CAREER GIRL: Goodness, they don't sound like good husbands at all! I'm glad they don't all stay that way.

PSYCHOANALYST: They don't. By the end of the third year and lasting until about the sixth year, both the oral and anal phases become subordinate to the phallic; that is, the center of pleasure shifts from mouth to anus, and thence to the penis.

HOUSEWIFE: Pardon me for asking, but just how does that apply to girls? After all . . .

PSYCHOANALYST: The girl's organ of sexual excitement during this period is the clitoris, which, as you ought to remember from elementary biology, corresponds to the penis and develops from the same bit of tissue in the fetus. This phase is exceedingly important in Freudian theory, involving as it does the desire for sexual connection with the opposite-sex parent. It's the period which sees the development of the Oedipus complex—the keystone of Freud's theory of sexuality in children.

LAWYER: Why did Freud pick out the hero of an old Greek play? What could the Greeks have known about psychoanalysis?

PSYCHOANALYST: The legend of King Oedipus is the story of a man who couldn't escape his fate, part of which involved sexual possession of his mother. Oedipus was the son of Laius, the King of Thebes, and Jocasta, his wife. Since an oracle had informed Laius that his son would be his murderer, the child was put out on a mountain to die as soon as he was born. He was rescued by a Corinthian shepherd, adopted by the King of Corinth, and brought up as his son. When Oedipus, too, was told by an oracle that he would kill his father, he fled Corinth, thinking to escape the prophecy, since he believed the King of Corinth to be his father. In his wanderings he met a stranger, quarreled with him, and killed him, and that stranger was Laius, his real father. Next, by solving a riddle, he became King of Thebes and was given the hand of Jocasta, the Queen, though of course he didn't know she was his mother. Later, a terrible plague ravaged Thebes, and an oracle declared that only the banishment of the murderer of Laius would end it. When the truth was finally brought out, and Oedipus learned who he was and what he had done, Jocasta killed herself and Oedipus put out his eyes and went into exile.

LAWYER: A very gruesome story—but precisely what does it tell me about the Oedipus complex in modern psychology?

PSYCHOANALYST: Freud felt that this tale, no matter how beautifully told by Sophocles, could not have continued to grip modern audiences, who find tragedy not in fate, but in people's characters, unless there was something in it that we recognized as true for all of us. This he believed was every child's love for the parent of the opposite sex, and his wish to be rid of the parent of the same sex. He pointed out that Jocasta herself comforts

Oedipus—before either of them knows the truth, but is aware of the prediction concerning him—with the words:

For many a man has seen himself in dreams
His mother's mate, but he who shuts his mind
To such forbidden things is more content.

This supported Freud's growing conviction that such feelings were universal. More recently, to be sure, anthropologists, who have studied cultural differences and their effects on childhood conflicts, have sown some doubt about how truly universal the feeling is, but there is little question that these incestuous and parricidal impulses exist universally *within our culture,* as well as in the earlier civilizations which helped to shape it.

TEACHER: During the phallic period, then, the child's love is supposed to be directed away from the self and toward the opposite parent?

PSYCHOANALYST: That's right. And it's a real love affair; for many, it is the most intense in their entire lives. You've all seen the violent hatred of a little boy as he says to his father, "I can beat you up." He means it, even if he knows it's wishful thinking. Sometimes a boy may tell his mother he's going to marry her when he grows up; sometimes he simply watches her when she's dressing; sometimes there is more or less veiled jealousy toward the father.

HOUSEWIFE: How true! There are times when I feel like the prize in a contest.

PSYCHOANALYST: Yes, the rivalry for the mother is clear to see; and if there are brothers and sisters, this is a time when the competition among them tends to be most intense, too. But Freud believed that the child, along with being jealous of his father, is also fearful of him, and afraid that his envy of his father's superior physical equipment, and his love for his father's mate, will bring a terrible retaliation.

LAWYER: Spankings? No dinner? How terrible a retaliation?

PSYCHOANALYST: The worst of all—castration. Little boys specifically fear to be deprived of the very thing that makes them rivals of their fathers. This fear is frequently reinforced by the discovery that little girls don't have penises. Boys are often sure that girls once had, but lost, this precious possession. In addition, there are often veiled or even overt threats by parents at their children's masturbation, such as, "You'll harm it by doing that," or "If you do that it will get sick and fall off."

HOUSEWIFE: So that's why little boys clutch their penises when they're frightened!

PSYCHOANALYST: Quite likely. Now the point in all this is that, as Freud saw it, this emerging fear of castration is the primary factor in the resolution of the Oedipus complex. It induces the boy to transfer his attachment for his mother to other objects, and thus solves what seemed to be an impossible conflict within the family.

LAWYER: The whole thing sounds pretty farfetched to me.

PSYCHOANALYST: The Oedipus complex was the most controversial part of Freud's theory, I think, and even today many intelligent people cannot quite accept it. But we believe this is so precisely because these wishes are so strongly repressed that most of us cannot remember ever having had them. The impulses were so powerful, and aroused such feelings of guilt, that we cannot bear to recall them. But there have been innumerable examples given by patients during analysis—as well as by normal people, in clinical studies—of dreams in which, in disguised form, they kill the parent of the same sex or have intercourse with the parent of the opposite sex. All of us, in fact, have such wish-fulfilling dreams, though we usually fail to see through the disguising symbolism.

TEACHER: But how does all this work in the case of the girl? You said that she, too, loves her father and hates her mother, but surely she doesn't suffer from the little boy's kind of fear. How does she resolve the incestuous dilemma?

PSYCHOANALYST: Freud thought that the first object of attachment of both boys and girls is the mother, but that when the little girl realizes that she doesn't have a penis, she becomes filled with feelings of shame, inferiority, and jealousy, and becomes furious with her mother for having permitted her to be born so incompletely. Thus she can transfer her affection toward her father.

CAREER GIRL: That sounds like the old penis-envy theory; I thought it wasn't accepted today.

PSYCHOANALYST: Freud's world *was* a man's world, and his

theory did seem to be borne out by the analyses of his patients. But today, when women are not considered the inferior creatures they were in the last century, woman's envy of man is not so all-embracing, and the inevitability of penis envy is in question. Karen Horney and certain other eminent analysts have held that a girl's masculine strivings are due to a culture in which the male is more important than the female, and that the penis envy is only a symbolic term, while her attachment to her father is simply a natural physiological development.

LAWYER: Well, whether Freud or Horney was right, the problem still remains: how does a little girl get over her desire to marry her father? She couldn't very well be weaned away from it by a fear of being castrated.

PSYCHOANALYST: As a matter of fact, Freud felt that the little girl's love for her father lasted much longer than the boy's for his mother exactly because that fear is absent. He believed that it fades slowly, partially out of a realization of her father's lack of interest in her as a substitute for her mother, and partially because of the attitude of the world around her toward incest, a taboo she is certainly aware of by the time she's an adolescent. And there is still another cause, one which affects both boys and girls. Another phase follows the phallic period.

LAWYER: What could be left now that we've gone through all the pleasure organs?

PSYCHOANALYST: Well asked! During the sixth year there is a gradual disappearance of the child's earlier sexual drives and curiosity, and a decreasing interest in libidinous pleasure. Encouraged by his parents and stimulated by school, the child becomes interested in the surrounding world and in external objects. This period of latency, as it is known, lasts until puberty. Then sexual impulses reassert themselves—this time, however, assuming a more adult form as glandular changes take place. Repressions haunt the adolescent, however, who, though biologically capable, still has to prove himself. So it is that competitive school games, the swaggering in front of girls, the shyness, all tend to distinguish this period of life, and the sexual impulses at first have no clear object. But given time and a normal upbringing, what is called the genital personality emerges, and the capacity for mature love does develop.

TEACHER: And all this—the love of sucking, and defecation, and one's parents—is the work of the libido, the sexual drive that each of us is born with?

PSYCHOANALYST: Yes, but there's a good deal more to it than that, as Freud himself realized. He began, it is true, by believing that pleasure was the aim of man's life, and that the libido was the force which tried to achieve that aim. But during his lifetime he found the hypothesis too limited, and that too many facts simply didn't fit in. Since he was always an honest as well as an imaginative man, he eventually evolved a theory which took the new facts into consideration.

TEACHER: What were these new facts?

PSYCHOANALYST: In particular, during the First World War it was found that soldiers who became neurotic as a result of their war experiences had dreams not easily explained by Freud's theory. In their dreams they tended to relive their recent shocking experiences, and Freud felt that this could not be interpreted, like other dreams, as sexual wish fulfillment. He also noted that some cases of hostile and aggressive behavior—like suicides by painful poison or the bayoneting of men by men—could not be explained as expressions of the libido. Besides, he saw that there was a tendency for people to get into the same types of difficulty repeatedly —that a girl with a cruel mother, for example, would keep forming attachments to other women which would give her the same painful reactions she had had with her mother. In other words, there seemed to be a tendency to repeat earlier experiences automatically and without a change in reaction, whether the experience was pleasant or painful. He named this tendency repetition-compulsion, and felt that it was a *true* compulsion—an instinctual drive. By 1920 his ideas of a new theory of the instincts became crystallized and were described in *Beyond the Pleasure Principle*.

TEACHER: He didn't give up his idea of infantile sexuality, did he?

PSYCHOANALYST: Oh, no. But he proposed that there were two instincts, existing side by side, the sexual and the aggressive, and that they both participate in all our mental activities.

CAREER GIRL: Do you mean the life and death instinct?

PSYCHOANALYST: Freud called them that, although today we have dropped that usage pretty much. They are also referred to as the love instinct and the hate instinct. But the aggressive drive, whatever it is called, is a destructive one, whether it is turned inward upon oneself or directed against others, according to Freud. He also believed that both drives are present constantly, interacting with one another, so that sometimes the aggressive impulses are stronger, sometimes the love impulses. Take John Brown, for example, who fought so hard against slavery for twenty years. He certainly loved the Negroes. Yet he allowed his wife to live in terrible poverty on a bleak Adirondack farm while he fought his own private war, and when his sons were old enough to be of use to him he made them join him, and no pleading or suffering on their part deterred him. Was that love? And when he was finally hanged, his lawyer said of him that he "wants to hang! Heaven save his soul, the old man *wants* to hang!"

HOUSEWIFE: If libido means the sex drive, is there a similar word for the aggressive drive?

PSYCHOANALYST: No. In fact, there has been a general misuse of the word "libido" so that very frequently it is used to refer to the energy of both drives. This probably happened because for so many years Freud felt that the libido was the *only* drive.

TEACHER: Even two drives or instincts don't offer me a really satisfactory explanation of the human character.

PSYCHOANALYST: There were many dissatisfied theoreticians. And Freud was one of them. But he was working in brand-new territory, and he developed his ideas very slowly, as he compiled more information. Indeed, it wasn't until 1923—thirty years after his first publications on psychoanalysis—that he proposed his theory of the structure of the total personality, containing the id, the ego, and the superego.

TEACHER: Did this negate his earlier instinct theory?

PSYCHOANALYST: No, but it changed the emphasis from a biological to an environmental one, and made room for much of our present-day awareness of social influences. As he saw it, the personality is divided into three parts—the id, the ego, and the superego. Of course, this is no physical division, and you won't find a special place in the body for any of these parts, any more than you will for the conscious and the unconscious. But this division indicates the different functions and the way they interact, according to Freud. The first part, the id, is the part we are born with, and it represents all the ungoverned impulses and desires of our instincts.

HOUSEWIFE: Why is it called the id?

PSYCHOANALYST: That's a Latin word meaning "it." It indicates the impersonal, the part of us dominated by nature. The id is chaotic; the impulses within it are completely disconnected from each other and from the environment. So a newborn infant sucks, cries, eliminates—whatever his id demands. But from the moment of birth, he begins to acquire knowledge and experience. Accordingly, the ego, the integrating part of the personality, begins to develop. It learns that the mother's breast comes with mother, so it sees to it that baby loves mother, and learns to wait more or less patiently until mother is available. It learns that the stove is hot, and doesn't let the child go on getting burned. It finds out that milk tastes better than an old shoe, and makes its choice accordingly. As the child grows older and a new baby comes along, it is the ego which discovers that the id's desire to get rid of the new baby would not go over at all well with mother, and so the child prevents itself from doing what it would dearly love to do. In other words, the ego's job is to modify, select, control, and coordinate the tendencies of the id, and to exclude those impulses which are in conflict with external reality. And it is the ego which *distinguishes* between the outside world and the inner impulses of the id.

CAREER GIRL: Does the ego act consciously?

PSYCHOANALYST: In large part. Some of its functions, like directing eating, or reading, or concluding from seeing the sun shining that it is day rather than night, are obviously conscious. But repression, among other ego functions, is not. When the ego buries a desire to have sexual relations with one's brother, it is acting unconsciously, at the behest of the third part of the personality—the superego.

CAREER GIRL: I thought the superego was one's conscience.

PSYCHOANALYST: So it has been called.

CAREER GIRL: And it operates unconsciously?

PSYCHOANALYST: We can't consciously control the influence of the superego. The boy who has been brought up to "respect his elders" can't, as a man, contradict an older person or a superior without feelings of anxiety. This is because the superego embodies the opinions and values which the child has adopted from those people most influential in his earlier years. These are usually his parents, of course, and their opinions—and the respect for authority, if that's what they built into him—become part of the child's personality, inflexible, unconscious. They become, in fact, the parent to the rest of the personality. But at the same time he is conscious of his conscience, because the opinions and values of his parents reflect the point of view of the culture in which they live, so that he continually hears and talks about what is "right" and "good."

CAREER GIRL: You say the superego is inflexible. You mean it doesn't change with experience?

PSYCHOANALYST: Very little. The ego is the adaptable part of the personality. It tries to make life as pleasant as possible, by giving way to the desires of the id whenever such desires won't conflict with the demands of reality. When the id wants to eat, the ego looks over the food situation, and if there's food available that won't harm the individual, it says go ahead. But the superego cannot do this. If that food has a speck of dirt or a hair on it, and the individual has been brought up to be a neat, clean person, the superego won't let him eat it. The ego might try to reason that one little speck won't hurt, but the superego will make the person's stomach turn over at the thought. The superego is almost completely out of touch with contemporary reality; its force is based on childhood concepts and the authority of ancient standards. It has a child's concept of justice. You eat something you shouldn't, something dirty, it says, and you'll be sick. Nor can the superego discriminate between the wish and the deed. The superego threatens punishment for the one almost as severely as for the other, and thus the nausea at the mere sight of the forbidden food, as well as at the actual eating of it.

LAWYER: Why should that be?

PSYCHOANALYST: Because the precepts of the superego are most forcefully laid down in the personality at the age of four or five, or even younger, and the reactions to such training are those of a child of that age, who can't yet distinguish very clearly between fantasy and reality. He is to a large degree dominated by the belief that wishing makes it so.

TEACHER: Do you mean that the superego punishes the rest

of the personality? And for desires only, as well as acts?

PSYCHOANALYST: It can happen, yes. Let's say a boy wants his father to die so that he can marry his mother. This wish is, of course, repressed. But the superego, which forced the ego to bury the desire, still insists on punishment for it, like a dog who goes on snarling after the intruder has skulked away. The result to the man may be only occasional feelings of guilt, when, for example, a business rival dies; but if the repression is less successful, some suffering or self-injury may be unconsciously arranged for, such as a failure in his career or an automobile accident. As a matter of fact, Freud pointed out that a person's criminal career may begin as a result of a need for punishment.

LAWYER: That kind of unreasoning authority sounds very dangerous.

PSYCHOANALYST: It certainly is. And that is why the ego tries to placate the superego as well as the id.

HOUSEWIFE: How does it do that?

PSYCHOANALYST: In a variety of ways, some of them socially useful, some harmful. Take, for example, voyeurism. Every child is somewhat voyeuristic, but this tendency diminishes as the need for it decreases. In some individuals, though, the need is unusually strong, and remains; such a person for his own psychic comfort may grow up to be a strong supporter of an antivice society, zealous in seeking out dealers in obscene pictures. Naturally his activities involve his continually looking for pictures of naked men and women. You see how he has solved this problem for himself. He satisfies his desire to look at naked ladies, and absolves himself from the feelings of guilt which his superego demands by "projecting" the desire and the guilt onto others. Whenever the repressed desires rise up toward consciousness, and are sniffed by the watchdog superego, more drastic defenses become necessary. One of these is to attribute the repressed tendencies to others—we call that "projection." Perhaps the feeling is hatred; then the distortion would be: "He wants to attack me, *I* don't want to attack *him*."

CAREER GIRL: That sounds like paranoia.

PSYCHOANALYST: Such projection *can* be the basis of delusions of persecution. But in the neurotic, projection is a kind of imperfect way to save the personality from serious mental illness. Repression is supposed to keep forbidden desires of the id out of sight, but if it fails to do so completely, the individual is in real danger unless he musters other defenses, and projection is just such an activity.

LAWYER: Are there still other defenses?

PSYCHOANALYST: Yes, one of the most common measures is the development of character traits exactly opposite to the original impulse. This is known as "reaction formation." Repressed cruelty can be kept unconscious by exaggerated compassion for the suffering of others. The early frowned-upon desire to play with one's feces might lead to excessive cleanliness and disgust at dirt. Another measure is "rationalization."

TEACHER: You mean self-deception?

PSYCHOANALYST: Not necessarily. That's the ordinary meaning of it. We have a somewhat special meaning. You see, a man may give a very large sum of money to fight leukemia because he wants to help humanity, because he desires prominence, or because he wants to relieve the guilt feeling he's acquired by his heartless methods of doing business. His rationalization may be that he wants to help his community, and this explanation permits the repression of the less savory motives. After all, all human acts are motivated by a number of considerations.

There are still other actions the ego may take, including turning the impulse inward. Thus cruelty might become masochism, in which pleasure is derived from receiving pain. We discussed another possible outcome of this action when we talked about the cause of depressions.

LAWYER: The ego seems to fight a defensive battle every minute.

PSYCHOANALYST: Well, Freud believed that one's character was formed by the defenses of the ego. But it isn't as negative as it sounds. The ego, after all, is the great compromiser. And several of the ways it satisfies the id, the superego, and the environment have a very positive, healthy effect on the personality. One of these is the way the child identifies himself with his parents and their attitudes. I'm sure you've smiled at the little girl who cuddles her doll just as her mother cuddles the new baby. That little girl's ego may be protecting her against a desire to push her baby sister off her mother's lap, but she is nevertheless learning what society expects of her, and she will grow up to love children quite adequately. Then I'm sure you all know how important sublimation is in producing the mature, social personality.

LAWYER: I thought sublimation meant taking a cold shower because you couldn't go to bed with a girl. That doesn't sound very social.

PSYCHOANALYST: You're mistaken, however. Freud recognized that the drives, both aggressive and sexual, aim only at their own satisfaction. But life isn't one long orgy of selfish satisfaction. Freud believed that the ego in a mature personality was able to provide the id with adequate gratification by diverting the energy of the drives into socially acceptable and even desirable behavior. Sometimes this can be seen very clearly—as with the surgeon or the butcher who saves or feeds people while obviously gratifying his desire to cut or wound; or the sculptor who molds statues instead of playing with feces. But there are many other not so clear aspects of sublimation which are nevertheless present and praiseworthy—sports, games, politics, business, friendship are all areas where sublimation has made selfish impulses acceptable both to the individual and the world around him.

TEACHER: It all sounds so hopeless. If your character is determined so early in life, and so greatly by your parents' attitudes, it doesn't seem worthwhile trying to change anything. It's all someone else's fault and no decision is really your responsibility.

PSYCHOANALYST: You are not alone in that reaction. Many people since Freud have felt that he placed too much emphasis on the importance of the drives, and that his theory of character development was too much influenced by his new knowledge of the importance of the early years and the unconscious. Today, indeed, I would say that most analysts give credit to the environment for a much greater and continuing influence on one's character.

TEACHER: But his theory *was* accepted at the time?

PSYCHOANALYST: On the contrary, as with all his ideas, it was accepted at first only by a very few brilliant men who worked with him to expand them. When his first books were published at the very beginning of the twentieth century, they shocked and repelled most people. But because they revealed certain hidden truths, they had an inexorable effect. In 1906 two psychiatrists, Eugen Bleuler and Carl Jung, began to apply Freud's theories in their Swiss clinic. In 1908 the first psychoanalytic congress met and founded a journal to spread the word. The men who met at that time, and others who came later to gather around Freud, were the pioneers. And a fascinating lot they were.

HOUSEWIFE: Who were they? Would I know their names?

PSYCHOANALYST: Only a few of them. And there were really too many for me to discuss them tonight. I might just mention the major ones. Jung, for instance—

CAREER GIRL: I had always thought Jung was a mystic, not a scientific physician.

PSYCHOANALYST: It's true that he never really accepted Freud's belief in the importance of the sexual drive, and by 1912 he had theorized that the source of the neurosis was to be found in a struggle with a "collective" unconscious, derived from the past experiences of the whole race. He did, however, make a good many contributions, among which was the particularly influential concept of the extroverted and introverted types.

TEACHER: I've always heard the name of Adler linked to that of Jung.

PSYCHOANALYST: That may be because they were contemporaries, and both were early followers of Freud. But Alfred Adler was a Viennese physician, who joined the original psychoanalytic group that used to meet informally on Wednesday evenings around the table in Freud's waiting room in 1907.

CAREER GIRL: He's the man who coined the phrase "inferiority complex," isn't he?

PSYCHOANALYST: He is. He believed that the struggle for power dominates man's behavior and that everyone has feelings of inferiority which stem from his childhood.

TEACHER: Didn't Adler, too, reject Freud's ideas?

PSYCHOANALYST: Yes, he was so taken with the idea of the importance of the struggle against inferiority that he looked upon the sexual drive itself as largely a competitive struggle with the outside world. Moreover, he placed so much emphasis on the pursuit of goals that he minimized the importance of the libido and of repressed conflicts, and this led Freud to feel that Adler denied the existence of the unconscious. At any rate, they separated, and Adler eventually established his own school of thought.

LAWYER: You don't seem to feel that either of these men deserved to join the firm.

PSYCHOANALYST: Well, some of their theories are now part of the body of psychoanalytic knowledge, for they were both highly intelligent men, but neither man's whole system of thought has ever been widely accepted.

TEACHER: How about the other early disciples? Did they all break away?

PSYCHOANALYST: Far from it. There were many followers who remained with Freud, and contributed a great deal to the mainstream of psychoanalysis. I've mentioned Karl Abraham; then there was Sandor Ferenczi, who was noted for his experiments in the technique of psychoanalysis; Georg Groddeck, who contributed the original concept of the id; Otto Fenichel and Ernest Jones, who, besides original research, compiled what was known about psychoanalysis; and many others.

TEACHER: I find it interesting that the names of the dissenters are better known. Rank, for instance, whom you haven't mentioned, is certainly a better-known name than Abraham.

PSYCHOANALYST: The creator of an idea is always better known than the one who carries ideas forward and develops them. And it was when these dissenters were also creators, with worthwhile ideas, that they were memorable. Besides, it was the differences of opinion that moved psychoanalysis forward, especially in those early days when Freud himself was altering and developing his ideas. As for Otto Rank, by the way, he was a particularly influential man, who was closely associated with Freud for more than twenty years. And when he finally broke away, after a series of disagreements, Freud was very grieved.

HOUSEWIFE: What did they disagree about?

PSYCHOANALYST: Rank developed a new theory of personality and will, in which he emphasized that the individual could act decisively, independent of outside influences or inner drives. He developed this will theory in connection with a new approach to therapy, which was very much needed in the twenties, since psychoanalysis had begun to grow quite theoretical. I don't have time to discuss his technique; but I will say that although there were hazards in his methods, he had a very large part in awakening psychoanalysts to the importance of the relationship between the doctor and his patient, and of trying to improve the techniques of psychoanalysis.

LAWYER: How about today? I bet there's many an analyst who raises a relevant objection.

PSYCHOANALYST: Of course. We wouldn't want it any other way.

HOUSEWIFE: And have there been a good many accepted changes of theory and technique?

PSYCHOANALYST: I haven't tried to do more than hint at how much growth and change there was in Freud's ideas during his lifetime. I have presented them to you very much as they are accepted today. His theory of the unconscious and his discovery of the source of neurosis in repressed conflicts are still the foundation for psychoanalysis. But there have certainly been modifications both in theory and in technique. One factor that has been of the utmost importance in its effect on every analyst's thinking is the fairly recent interest in anthropology and sociology, and in the variability of human personality in differing cultures. Back in the thirties, certain anthropologists—Ruth Benedict was perhaps the best known of them—began to point out how differently other peoples behave, and what varied forms so-called "normality" can take, in disconnected cultures; she and others thus began to correct the parochial and shortsighted views of psychoanalytic theorists. Psychoanalysts began to pay more heed to the relationship of man to his social environment, and the interaction of men and customs, and their ability to change each other.

TEACHER: The anthropologists and sociologists offered these new perspectives, you say—but why did psychoanalysts listen to them? Aren't all professions conservative about outside influences?

PSYCHOANALYST: Of course, but there were a few active pioneers within psychoanalysis who espoused the new ideas, offered theories to incorporate them, and so brought social science inside psychoanalysis. Three of the most influential people were Karen Horney, Erich Fromm, and Harry Stack Sullivan. Their theories are still being argued today, although Horney's first book came out in the thirties.

CAREER GIRL: What are the arguments about?

PSYCHOANALYST: Horney, for one—she, by the way, was an orthodox Freudian practicing psychoanalyst for over fifteen years before the publication of her own theory—placed so much emphasis on environment as the cause of neurosis as to imply that the stresses of society can operate apart from the forces of the instincts, and that the past life of the patient is of little consequence. This point of view had a tremendous effect on her method of treatment, naturally, and that, too, is still being hotly debated today, years after her death.

TEACHER: And what are the objections to Fromm and Sullivan?

PSYCHOANALYST: Again, it's a question of emphasis. Both men believe—Sullivan, I should add, is dead—that man's character and neuroses are formed by the interacting influences of other people, and both tend to minimize the importance of the instincts. Neither, however, denies the importance of the early life of the patient, or the way our unconscious operates in spite of our conscious desires.

TEACHER: Which of these men you've mentioned is represented by a school of psychoanalysis?

PSYCHOANALYST: I prefer not to use the term "school of psychoanalysis." At an earlier time, to be sure, it may have had a lot more significance than it has now. But though there are certainly training institutions in operation today with widely varying theoretical orientations—Freudian, Adlerian, Jungian, Sullivanian, to name a few—and the therapeutic techniques they teach *do* differ, psychoanalysis has been altered by many people's ideas, and in actual practice psychoanalysts appear to differ more as individuals than as representatives of specific theories and techniques.

HOUSEWIFE: I don't understand what part of these theories is considered psychoanalysis and what is not.

PSYCHOANALYST: That's not surprising, since psychoanalysis is so constantly changing. But let me try to indicate the *sina qua non* of both the theory and the technique: In everyone there are unconscious psychological processes which play an important role in determining much of our behavior. When they become dominant, however—that is, in neurosis—the way a person thinks and acts can't be changed to any important degree without changing his unconscious processes. Psychoanalysis, therefore, tries to change his behavior by revealing and altering the unconscious ideas which control him. It does this, fundamentally, in two principal ways—first, by the skillful use of the relationship between patient and analyst, which we call the "transference," and second, by uncovering, resolving, and mastering the obstacles, known as resistances, which the unconscious sets up to defend itself. When the uncovering and redirection of unconscious forces is held to be unnecessary, the term "psychoanalysis" should not be applied; but so long as the treatment is undertaken on these basic assumptions, the techniques used may vary, or be augmented, or even be considerably altered, and yet the therapy can be said still to be psychoanalysis.

CHAPTER FIVE

CHOOSING THE ANALYST

*How to check his qualifications; what his training should in-
clude; lay vs. medical analysts; why the analyst must be
analyzed; fees and sessions; the significance of personal traits.*

PSYCHOANALYST: Let's assume that you have discovered, by
the process of elimination, that you need the help of a psychoanalyst. You are not rich and bored; you are suffering. Perhaps
you can't get to work on time, or you're driven by some senseless
compulsion, or you can't concentrate on your work, or your heart
and mind feel walled away from the rest of the world. And the
unreasonable feelings of panic and anxiety which cover your forehead with beads of perspiration, make your knees tremble, your
heart pound, and your breath fail have not been eased by all the
exhortations of well-meaning friends. Your minister, too, finds
your troubles beyond his scope, and your doctor can't help you.
We're also going to assume that you have not been to a social
agency or a mental health clinic; if you had, someone there would
probably have given you a specific referral to a psychoanalyst.
Human nature being what it is, you have probably asked around
among your friends and been given the names of several analysts
who helped them or their friends.

HOUSEWIFE: Well, don't we all ask friends to recommend their
own doctors?

PSYCHOANALYST: Indeed we do. And at least it's better, in my
field, than trying to find someone by looking in the yellow pages,
where a fellow can list himself as a psychoanalyst as long as he
can spell the word.

LAWYER: You seem to be implying that the recommendation of a friend is a poor way to choose an analyst, however.

PSYCHOANALYST: It's an adequate beginning, but you should do some checking before making a selection. First, you must ask yourself if this friend has really been helped by the psychoanalyst he recommended. Moreover, the analysis would have to be completed, or at least well advanced, before you could really judge the improvement; otherwise you might be confused by conflicting reports about an analyst. One acquaintance, in the early untroubled stages, might praise him highly, and another, who has abandoned treatment when it got unpleasant, might dismiss him contemptuously. So once you know that your friend's analysis has been completed, you must ask yourself if he comes closer to that mentally healthy individual we described several weeks ago than he did before his analysis. You must know what he was like before and after treatment; if he's a hard-driving, ambitious man now, who's dropped most of his old friends, you must know whether his former passivity contained any real love for all those friends, for instance, or whether he experienced only loneliness, frustration, and hatred when he was in the privacy of his own room. You must also know whether he completed treatment to the satisfaction of his psychoanalyst before you are able to pass judgment. All this information is not easy to come by, unfortunately, unless you're on quite intimate terms with the ex-patient.

TEACHER: How true. It sounds like a Herculean task. What do we do without such proof?

PSYCHOANALYST: There are ways, luckily, in which you can check on the psychoanalyst himself. And I believe very strongly that you should do this checking anyway, even if the recommended analyst has so far met the challenge of having successfully treated your friend. After all, there's a good deal to be said for the susceptibility of some individuals to miracle cures and placebos, and your friend might conceivably have been helped by an unqualified person. But since statistically your chances are better with science than magic, I suggest that you check the man's background and training. For that matter, I think you might want to do some checking even if you've gotten the recommendation from your family doctor—most G.P.'s aren't close enough to the subject to have expert opinions on it.

HOUSEWIFE: How do we check up on the analyst?

PSYCHOANALYST: There are various associations to which reputable men belong, and frequently the education and clinical experience of the members are included in membership lists published by these organizations. Even if you don't know the affiliation of the analyst you're interested in, or how good the association is, you can usually get all this information by a phone call to your county mental health association, local health or social welfare department, county medical society, a family service agency or mental health clinic, or the psychology department of the nearest college.

HOUSEWIFE: And suppose you don't have a recommendation from a friend?

PSYCHOANALYST: In that case, many of these same sources will make recommendations. Or you can choose the simple and fairly reliable method of writing directly to one of the organizations which admit only psychoanalytic psychotherapists.* In this way you'll avoid confusion with psychologists and psychiatrists who do not have private practices in psychoanalysis. There are a number of such highly specialized associations, and although not every analyst is a member of one of these specific groups, membership in one of them does indicate that the practitioner's character and training have been scrutinized and approved before admittance. All these organizations publish lists of their members; they will send you either the complete list or the names of practitioners in your area.

TEACHER: Why is it necessary that the man be a member of one of these associations? Can't you go to his office and see his diplomas?

PSYCHOANALYST: Unfortunately, there are a large number of unaccredited schools—diploma mills, they're aptly called—which, even by correspondence courses alone, offer diplomas and doctoral degrees in philosophy, psychology, science, psychotherapy, or the like. One school, which was mentioned in a report on the subject in *American Psychologist*, grants a Ph.D. after only eighteen months of study, without any previous college education.

TEACHER: And what does it mean if the analyst does belong to one of the reputable associations?

* See Appendix B for names and addresses of these organizations.

PSYCHOANALYST: If he is a qualified practicing analyst—I say "if" because some of the members of many fine organizations are not, but are rather psychologists or nonanalytic psychiatrists or simply educators in the field—if, however, he is listed as a practicing analyst, you can be confident that he will have adequate knowledge and skills to treat you. He will have an understanding of other fields of learning, especially the behavioral sciences, such as anthropology and sociology, as well as his rigorous analytic training. He will be equipped to combine dispassionate knowledge with human feeling.

You may know the story of an old man lying in the hospital, in the last stages of cancer, cadaverous, pallid, and semiconscious from the morphine administered to relieve the pain. In comes a group of medical students, who stand around him and discuss his appearance and condition in cold, scientific terms. Then a group of liberal arts students is shown the same patient. Their reactions are quite different, however. They stand there silently, feeling a mixture of horror and pity while they try to arrive at a philosophic appraisal of life. The analyst has the qualities of both kinds of students. He is genuinely concerned and sympathetic with his troubled patients, but he is, at the same time, able to examine objectively their symptoms and their behavior, and, through understanding, help free them from crippling blocks, distortions, and anxieties.

TEACHER: What kind of training leads to that mingling of qualities? Is it much the same whatever school the analyst goes to?

PSYCHOANALYST: No, it isn't. The first training institute in this country—that of the New York Psychoanalytic Society—has only been in existence since 1923, which is a comparatively short time ago, and there are still considerable differences among the institutes that have sprung up since then. In part this is because of theoretical orientation—that is, a leaning either toward strict Freudian concepts or toward an acceptance of other points of view—and in part because of a difference in emphasis on academic courses or actual experience. A fairly uniform sort of training is offered by the nineteen training centers approved by the American Psychoanalytic Association, but this education is in the classical Freudian tradition, and the Association does not approve or even evaluate schools which, for example, emphasize Sullivan's or Horney's contributions. These nineteen approved schools have stringent prerequisites for admission, which include graduation from a Grade A medical school and a residency in psychiatry. The curriculum includes courses, seminars, and clinical conferences extending over at least a three-year period; no less than two supervised analyses of patients by the student; and the student's own analysis. One may attend these schools without being a psychiatrist, but such an individual is expected to refrain from the private practice of psychoanalysis, and he will not be accepted into membership in the Association even upon completion of all the training.

TEACHER: Is there other training, then, available to the non-physician who wants to become an analyst?

PSYCHOANALYST: Yes, there are a number of institutes which offer somewhat similar training without having the medical degree as a requisite for admission. For example, the National Psychological Association for Psychoanalysis, an institute in New York City, admits candidates who have had graduate work in one of the studies of human behavior, such as psychology or social work. It offers them academic courses in psychiatry, the history, theory and technique of psychoanalysis, and the study of recent developments such as group therapy, plus practical workshop courses and case presentations and conferences. It requires, too, that each student have the very necessary personal training analysis as well as the practical experience of treating patients under the supervision of control analysts.

LAWYER: And do graduates become members of the Association?

PSYCHOANALYST: Yes, but the National Psychological Association for Psychoanalysis is not an over-all organization which prescribes standards for the whole profession, as the American Psychoanalytic Association is for medical psychoanalysts. It is only one of a number of such organizations in the area of lay analysis. Consequently, it's much more difficult to check on the training of a nonmedical analyst.

LAWYER: If proper training does exist for lay analysts, why the aura of fraudulence that surrounds the term?

PSYCHOANALYST: There are two reasons why lay analysts have been suspect. For one thing, only about a third of the states have laws governing even the designation of "psychologist." Nothing deters anyone from calling himself a psychoanalyst, but the medical analyst is subject to the disciplines of the medical profession. This situation is being changed, however. A growing umbrella organization, under the leadership of the Council of Psychoanalytic Psychotherapists, believes that since it would be difficult to provide adequate protection to the public through state legislation, a council of professional organizations should work together to assure high standards. To this end, the Council of Psychoanalytic Psychotherapists has so far affiliated with four other associations. It is, of course, open to both lay and medical psychotherapists—although only a limited number of the latter have joined thus far—and the public can at least feel confident about the qualifications and ethics of a member of one of these affiliated groups.

The second reason for people's low opinion of lay analysts is that the public reflects the attitude of the medical profession, which has, for years, been campaigning against the practice of psychotherapy by medically unsupervised laymen, no matter how well trained.

TEACHER: Originally the medical profession was against all psychoanalysis, wasn't it?

PSYCHOANALYST: Yes, medical recognition of its value came slowly. By 1925, however, not only were physicians accepting psychoanalysis, but some of them began to contend that it should be the exclusive province of medicine. This idea was debated within the International Psychoanalytical Association from 1925 to 1939, at which time the American societies within the International decided to restrict their training institutes to physicians—or, as I mentioned, those nonphysicians who didn't intend to enter private practice. But not all the groups within the International did this. In Britain, for instance, nonphysicians are accepted in the British Psychoanalytic Society, the only proviso to their practice being that the initial diagnosis of a case must be made by a physician.

TEACHER: But Freud himself didn't think it was necessary for an analyst to be a doctor, did he?

PSYCHOANALYST: On the contrary, he even wrote a little book

in support of lay analysts, and discouraged some of his pupils from medical training.

CAREER GIRL: And he turned out some awfully good lay analysts, didn't he?

PSYCHOANALYST: Yes, Otto Rank, Theodor Reik and Anna Freud, Sigmund's daughter, are some of the better-known lay analysts. There's an ironic story in connection with this, too. In 1938, Theodor Reik, who has an international reputation as an analyst, arrived in New York as a refugee from Hitlerism. He expected, on the basis of his own renown as well as being Freud's pupil, to be welcomed into the New York Psychoanalytic Society; but since he wasn't a physician, the Society refused to offer him a regular membership. He began, therefore, to practice and to teach privately; then in 1947 a group of his pupils organized the National Psychological Association for Psychoanalysis, first as a membership society, and in 1950 as a training institute. And so there are undoubtedly many more nonmedical analysts in the United States today than there would have been if Reik had been welcomed into that local branch of the American Psychoanalytic Association.

TEACHER: But why should medical men feel so strongly that lay analysts shouldn't practice?

PSYCHOANALYST: Actually, they don't all feel that way, although it's the official view of the medical profession that all lay analysts should practice only under the direct supervision of physicians. Doctors feel that their long years of medical training, plus the very fact that they chose medicine as a vocation, have imbued them with a desire to cure, to heal; whereas nonmedical analysts, because of their background in the behaviorial sciences, have an intellectual approach which may underestimate the human need.

TEACHER: But social workers have no medical training either. Yet they are certainly filled with concern over the plight of troubled people, and are trained, as you admit, to help them.

PSYCHOANALYST: I agree with you. There *is* some validity in the argument, however. Then, too, doctors are afraid that lay analysts may not have a sufficient understanding of the organic problems that may be involved, and so may ignore their possible existence; or that they may be defensive about their nonmedical training and therefore loath to refer patients to a doctor.

CAREER GIRL: It seems to me that all specialists have their particular hobbyhorse, medical men or not, and gallop along on it, paying no attention to danger signals the patient's body may be sending out.

PSYCHOANALYST: I think you exaggerate. A competent specialist, though concerned with his own area only, sees to it that someone is looking after the rest of the person. Similarly, though a psychiatrist who practices analysis is theoretically able to diagnose and treat his patients for physical ailments as any M.D. is, practically none does. He will send his patient to another physician for an examination whenever he suspects the presence of a brain tumor, or thyroid deficiency, or any other physical trouble which yields psychological symptoms. And any new patient should have been examined first by another physician. The lay analyst should act in the same way, but may not be equipped to suspect such physical ailments. Still, the fear that some physical illness will be overlooked in the course of treatments does seem to me to be exaggerated by medical analysts, or at least by their public-relations committees.

HOUSEWIFE: Then in practice the medical and the lay analyst act in the same fashion?

PSYCHOANALYST: Yes, providing they have both had adequate training, they should be equally qualified. And considering that there are only somewhere around a thousand medical analysts and perhaps the same number of qualified lay analysts, who all together can hardly carry a caseload of more than 25,000 to 40,000 patients, it seems regrettable to engage in a jurisdictional dispute at this time. Let's hope that very shortly a training or certification program will be worked out to the satisfaction of both medical and nonmedical analysts. Then perhaps this country will have a greater supply of properly trained psychoanalysts without their having to spend years to become fully qualified psychiatrists first.

CAREER GIRL: And meanwhile are there two armed camps, with the poor patient caught in the crossfire?

PSYCHOANALYST: Things aren't that bad. The Joint Commission on Mental Illness and Health, composed of thirty-six organizations, including the A.M.A. and the American Psychological Association, prepared a report for Congress in which it recommended that psychoanalysis be practiced only by those with special training and experience in it, and suggested that this apply not only to physicians but to other professional people as well. Despite the A.M.A.'s official position on lay analysis, this report was signed by representatives of all the participating organizations, published as *Action for Mental Health,* and its findings contributed importantly to President Kennedy's 1963 proposals to Congress for an expansion of mental health facilities.

TEACHER: You've been talking about the training of present-day analysts. But what of earlier men who were practicing before such formalized education was accepted?

PSYCHOANALYST: These men have reputations which can be easily verified by a phone call to the psychology department of a university, or to the local chapter of your mental health association. And such men will very likely be members of one of the associations I mentioned.

LAWYER: What sort of legal protection does a patient have thanks to his analyst's membership in one of these associations?

PSYCHOANALYST: The patient doesn't have *legal* protection except when the state has passed legislation to that effect. Thus analysts who are also physicians, or, as I said earlier, psychologists in some states, are responsible for their professional conduct by law. But reputable associations do have codes of ethics and committees to enforce them, and, if charges are brought against one of their members, may take any action from a reprimand to expulsion. The American Psychological Association, for example, recognizes complaints from either members or nonmembers, and if the charges are verified by an investigation, not only takes strong action, but notifies the membership of the result and which principle of its code of ethics was violated.

LAWYER: And just what does this slap on the wrist do to the analyst?

PSYCHOANALYST: Don't underestimate the importance of having a good reputation in a field where recommendation is so important. But you seem to feel that it is fear which keeps the psychoanalyst on his good behavior, like a criminal afraid of a jail sentence. The analyst, however, like the physician with his Hippocratic oath, has his own strong code of ethics which is inculcated during his training. Indeed, it is more rigid than the physician's, for he is expected to have no social or business contacts with the patient outside of the analysis, nor is he to attempt to expand his practice by social contacts with the friends and relatives of his patients, although this is perfectly proper for other physicians.

LAWYER: All right, I bow to your high moral standards. Now, let me return to a point you seemed to emphasize earlier. You spoke of a personal analysis being very necessary. Why is that? Doesn't an analyst learn enough about how the human mind works from his academic work or from the cases which he himself analyzes under supervision?

PSYCHOANALYST: What he has learned with his conscious mind is not enough. The analyst must be aware of his own unconscious feelings and blind spots in order to guard against their affecting his attitude and reactions toward his patients. Once he has been analyzed, he can listen to his patients objectively and judge the nature of their problems and his thinking will be less likely to be colored by his own unconscious tendencies, cravings, or distortions. You all must have met the kind of woman who so hates her husband that she attributes all problems to a similar source: when a friend complains of a headache, she will ask, "Has your husband been yelling at you?" or when another one bemoans her inadequate wardrobe, she will hint that the woman's husband is spending money on another woman. This kind of neurotic distortion of the facts would seriously hamper an analyst in his functioning if *he* were prey to it, but he combats such tendencies by constant *self-analysis*, based on his training analysis.

LAWYER: You said last week, though, that everyone can't be successfully analyzed. Surely that leaves room for a lot of neurotics who are practicing analysis today.

PSYCHOANALYST: No, because being successfully analyzed is one of the requisites for admission into a reputable psychoanalytic association. Generally, the training analysis has removed most of the analyst's neurotic tendencies, but where it hasn't, he is at least aware of and alert to them, and keeps them under control through continual self-analysis. Frequently, if in his own analysis he has overcome a problem similar to that of his patient, he might be particularly interested in and suited to that patient. At any rate, the analyst should know enough about his own feelings to be able to examine and understand them and use them productively in his work rather than be misled by them. If, in isolated cases, he finds that a patient's problem activates his own tendencies harmfully, he will recommend another analyst.

CAREER GIRL: And is it his own analysis which keeps him from having his head turned by all the ladies who tell him they adore him?

PSYCHOANALYST: That and experience. The analyst knows, first of all, that the love his patient feels is not really for him; it is a recapitulation of early childhood love. After a while, moreover, he recognizes that it is simply unreasonable to think that each of his female patients is falling in love with him for his own sake. But in order to treat them, what the analyst must do, and can do because he has been analyzed, is to understand why he feels the way he does about his patients, whether it's in reaction to their protestations of love or their snarling abuse.

CAREER GIRL: Then he does have feelings!

PSYCHOANALYST: Oh, he's only human—and fortunately so. But it's his responsibility to understand the feelings aroused in him by the patient's seductiveness or loathing. The examination of his own feelings, based on his training analysis, insulates him and protects him from responding as he did in student days— oversympathetically to clinging-vine patients, impatiently with miserable, taunting ones, thinking himself the Solomon or Adonis his patients claimed he was, or even becoming dictatorial, arbitrary, and controlling.

TEACHER: We've spent a considerable time on the training of the analyst. And I, certainly, recognize its importance. But surely there are other factors to be considered, too. Money, for instance. Could a poor teacher like me afford to go to a psychoanalyst?

PSYCHOANALYST: Money *is* a weighty consideration, but the fees most analysts charge are not large, considering the training involved. Analytic training alone, after the student's graduate degree, costs between $15,000 and $20,000, and sometimes as much as $35,000, because the personal training analysis and the supervised or control analysis must be paid for by the student and are always done by experienced, and therefore expensive, psychoanalysts.

HOUSEWIFE: How much do these top men get?

PSYCHOANALYST: That varies. In New York there are a few people who charge as much as $50 an hour, but in the rest of the country the fees, like the cost of living generally, are more moderate. Most psychoanalysts charge between $20 and $30 an hour, depending on their training and years of experience, but there are many who work for less. As one Washington analyst pointed out, in our nation's capital there are a fair number of analysts who charge only $15 an hour—and the plumbers there get $7.50 for the same time.

TEACHER: But the average analysis—if I can judge from the figures you give—would cost about ten thousand dollars. How could I afford that on my salary?

PSYCHOANALYST: Why do you feel it necessary to pay for treatment out of your income? After all, you wouldn't hesitate to dip into your savings for an operation, if it was necessary. Ordinarily, we prefer analysis to be paid for out of income, rather than savings, yet this is not a rigid rule. It can be viewed as an investment, as a college education is, which will pay dividends for the rest of your life, and you could consider borrowing the money for it, from a member of your family, perhaps, or a friend.

TEACHER: Won't a psychoanalyst reduce his fees or vary them a bit, according to the means of the patient?

PSYCHOANALYST: Sometimes—in fact, often. An analyst may treat a penniless student who pays him nothing, a schoolteacher who pays him $10 or $15 an hour, and a stockbroker who pays $35 an hour.

HOUSEWIFE: Does every analyst have some patients at reduced rates?

PSYCHOANALYST: Almost every analyst carries a few patients at lower fees or even for nothing, or gives part of his time without compensation to hospitals. And any analyst will try to make it possible for a person in need of treatment to get it. If he cannot take a patient because the patient can't afford his fee, he will try to recommend another doctor whose fees are lower. But no analyst can reduce his fee for every patient, or he would be unable to make a living at all.

LAWYER: I've heard that analysts won't treat people free of charge because it isn't good for the patient.

PSYCHOANALYST: Some analysts do argue that if the patient

makes no personal financial sacrifice the analysis is foredoomed to failure. You know the old saying: advice is worth what you pay for it. And indeed in our present society what we get for nothing we tend to hold of little value. Just recall your reaction to television, for instance. No matter how special the program, or talented the writer, or famous the stars, if you have something else to do that night, you feel no dismay about missing the show. Its value has been diminished by its lack of price.

LAWYER: That sounds like rationalization to me. Where is the sacrifice if a parent or a spouse pays for treatment? Surely you don't mean that every adolescent or married woman whose analysis is paid for by a parent or husband is a poor patient? I think you're just defending high fees.

PSYCHOANALYST: I don't defend the rigid maintenance of high fees; indeed, if the fee is too high and requires too great a struggle for the patient to pay it, it may become a hindrance to his analysis. But ideally, the patient *should* be responsible for the cost of his treatment, and it *should* represent a sacrifice of some sort. I myself had a patient whom I treated at a very low fee, in spite of the fact that he had wealthy parents who were eager to give him the money, because I felt that his paying for himself was critical to his recovery.

CAREER GIRL: Now that sounds like the exceptional case to me.

PSYCHOANALYST: I don't think so. But don't condemn the analyst for taking the family's money. If he charges a low fee to a patient whose family can pay more, he limits his ability to lower his fee for another patient who has no one to turn to.

HOUSEWIFE: Can't a person with less money have fewer sessions a week, so that he won't have to pay so large a sum in so short a time?

PSYCHOANALYST: This is one of the questions about money which must be settled at the outset, in a frank discussion of fees and finances before treatment begins. The classical position is that there should be a session every twenty-four hours, so that dreams and fantasies can be related before they're forgotten. But in actual practice, orthodox Freudians settle for four or five sessions a week, and in some cases even less. Certainly, with fewer sessions, the analyst will have to have greater skill, and there remains the danger that too much time will be spent simply relating events to bring the analyst up to date, and too little time with the unconscious. Nevertheless, how few hours weekly are accepted as a working arrangement depends on the individual analyst. Some very reputable men, trained in orthodox fashion, today will treat a patient analytically in only one or two hours per week.

LAWYER: I'll bet very few of them are willing to settle for one or two. There's no profit in that kind of business.

PSYCHOANALYST: You know, it's a fallacy to think that it's a financial advantage to the analyst to spend five hours a week with each patient, year after year. If the analyst could give the patient fewer appointments, he'd be able to charge somewhat more for each hour and see many more patients, his gross income would be greater, and the risks would be less, since the loss of any one patient would make little difference in his income. Think of the huge fee a surgeon can charge for each operation because it happens only once to the patient. Yet the surgeon spent no more time in training than the psychoanalyst.

TEACHER: I'm still thinking about the poor teacher, or someone else in his financial position. His income is limited, and his prospects for borrowing are poor. Isn't there someplace where he can receive treatment for less money than an analyst will charge him in private practice?

PSYCHOANALYST: There are clinics connected with the training institutes and mental hospitals where he would be required to pay far less money, although there, too, what he pays is based on his income.

HOUSEWIFE: But wouldn't you be receiving treatment from people who are still in training, in the same way that interns treat you in a general hospital when you can't afford your own doctor?

PSYCHOANALYST: Yes, usually, but the cases which are accepted for treatment through a clinic are supervised by a control analyst. So you would to some extent be in the hands of a man who confers constantly on your case with one of the most experienced psychoanalysts.

HOUSEWIFE: How could a person find such a clinic?

PSYCHOANALYST: Again, a call to your county mental health association might locate one, although there are only a small number of such institutes in the country. And, as with already trained analysts, there simply aren't enough analysts-in-training to go around.

LAWYER: No wonder the psychoanalysts can be so independent, and can charge you even when you have to break your appointment with them.

PSYCHOANALYST: It's true that a patient may be charged for every session, even if he has advised his analyst beforehand that he can't be there. And this is an understandable practice. The analyst, after all, has made a long-term arrangement "leasing" a certain number of hours to the patient and he cannot use them for anything else. But in addition to the fact that the analyst would be unfairly burdened by the loss of income, permission to skip payment would reinforce the patient's natural temptation to avoid sessions when things become difficult. If he weren't charged, the analyst would be offering him a financial inducement to escape the session and go off and enjoy himself. It would be like a child playing hookey to miss a test, and receiving movie money from the teacher when he does. Some analysts do permit an absence on twenty-four hours' notice, however. It's another aspect of the "contract" that should be discussed at the outset.

CAREER GIRL: All right, let's suppose we admit the product is good for you, and is not too expensive—but how about the packaging? Doesn't the analyst's personality count when we make our selection?

PSYCHOANALYST: Strangely enough, not very much. And it has even less significance as treatment progresses. You see, the analyst, to do his job properly, must be as unknown as possible to the patient. So it doesn't matter whether he is married or divorced, likes dogs or keeps turtles, or carves fertility figures or listens to Bach. None of these things is your concern, or should be allowed to affect your feeling for him.

HOUSEWIFE: Why is it important that he be unknown to the patient?

PSYCHOANALYST: You'll understand this better later on, but let me just say now that it's necessary throughout analysis that the patient's varying attitudes toward the analyst reflect only the patient's ideas. When an ordinarily polite young man becomes so furious at the analyst that he screams filthy abuse at him, the analyst must be sure the patient is really furious at something or someone else, not the analyst himself. And if the patient does know something about the analyst which he dislikes, it can easily color his attitude and so hinder the process of self-knowledge.

HOUSEWIFE: Perhaps he does have to be unknown, but surely, if I were planning to reveal myself to someone, I'd have to *like* him when I met him.

PSYCHOANALYST: Not really. You shouldn't actively dislike him —although there can be successful analyses even with that kind of beginning. A patient who hates an analyst from the very first— you must admit this seems irrational—may all the more easily reveal hostile feelings which might take months to uncover under other circumstances. But this is exceptional; for the most part an analyst faced with immediate hostility would refer the new patient to someone else. The patient *should,* however, feel comfortable with his prospective analyst at the initial interview, and believe that the man understands the problem, at least to some degree, and the patient should be optimistic about the outcome.

HOUSEWIFE: Aren't there any personal qualities an analyst should have?

PSYCHOANALYST: He should certainly be friendly, patient, understanding, and sensitive. And, as Karl Menninger is careful to emphasize, modest and humble.

HOUSEWIFE: Does it matter whether the analyst is a man or a woman?

PSYCHOANALYST: Usually not, because every patient reacts to the analyst at various points as though he were a number of different people, both men and women. There are a few exceptions in which the sex of the analyst may be important, but these are rarely predictable. In those cases it may become necessary, during the course of the analysis, for the patient to be sent to someone else, but that shouldn't influence your choice at the beginning.

CAREER GIRL: How about religion or background?

PSYCHOANALYST: These don't have to be similar, but it is important for the analyst to have a knowledge and understanding of the patient's own culture.

CAREER GIRL: Yes, I remember years ago hearing an anecdote about a patient describing a dream to an analyst who had recently come from Vienna and had a limited knowledge of English. The patient was talking about her pigeonhole desk, and the analyst didn't know the term at all, and was busy interpreting the dream in terms of birds and flight and captivity.

PSYCHOANALYST:　Well, that's unlikely today, but unfortunately there are some analysts whose middle-class, sheltered American backgrounds are so completely different from that of a first-generation European, for instance, that there would be unnecessary obstacles in the way of the analytic relationship. However, the analyst himself will be as aware of this as the patient, and the initial interview would disclose any such difficulties.

HOUSEWIFE:　Then on the basis of the first interview the patient and the psychoanalyst can make a decision?

PSYCHOANALYST:　No more than a temporary one. The first weeks or even months of analysis should be considered a trial period for both the patient and the analyst. During this time the analyst can make a careful study of the patient's illness and better evaluate the possibility of successful therapy. And not infrequently an analyst will be able to recognize even sooner the cases he can't help.

HOUSEWIFE:　And can the patient change his analyst if he finds he doesn't get along with him?

PSYCHOANALYST:　A patient can always change his analyst, but it's wise to try to discuss his feelings with his analyst first, to discover if the two people are incompatible or if the patient is simply running away from his own problems. The analyst's personality, you remember, becomes less and less important to the patient as he gets deeper into analysis, so the patient's dislike of him may be only a temporary reflection of some old feelings which are being revived. The patient should retain a feeling of confidence, however, and if he feels that he has learned nothing and that he is floundering and treatment has bogged down, he could certainly ask for an evaluation by another psychoanalyst. But if all the factors we've talked of are favorable, if the analyst has been properly trained and psychoanalyzed, and if he is the considerate, responsible human being I've described, it is unlikely that the patient will become so despairing that he feels the analysis is a failure. Rather, the chances are very good that the patient will remain confident, will continue to learn, and that his analysis will succeed.

IN THE BEGINNING

*How it starts; an unusual doctor-patient relationship; dos and
don'ts for the patient; advice for the family; the why and how
of free association; the interpretation and use of dreams.*

HOUSEWIFE: I've often wondered what it would be like to go
to a psychoanalyst. Are you shown into his private office by a
discreet, impersonal secretary? And does it look as it does in the
movies?

PSYCHOANALYST: Most analysts have no secretaries. They have
so few patients they don't need any. But the psychoanalyst's office
is depicted fairly accurately in movies and television. Physically,
it's very much like any consultation room—a desk and chairs,
lamps and ashtrays, books in the bookcases, pictures on the walls,
drapes at the windows. Sometimes there are diplomas attesting to
the man's education and right to practice. Only the addition of a
couch changes its aspect—and certainly you expect that. Perhaps
what a new patient doesn't expect, however, is a most important
furnishing—the atmosphere. He is received into a quiet, serene
haven, from which the world and its pressures seem remote, and
where he faces a calm, interested, friendly specialist.

LAWYER: Faces? I thought he lies down and does *not* face
him.

PSYCHOANALYST: Usually the first hour, or even several hours,
consist of face-to-face discussions, until the patient is relaxed or
comfortable enough to use the couch. During these first hours,
when they are facing each other, the analyst guides the conversation—but with a very light hand. He wants to know what is troubling the patient, which is usually just what the patient most

wants to tell. Or at least he wants to tell what he thinks is troubling him; in actual fact, a good many patients aren't really sure of what that is.

LAWYER: What do you mean? How can a person not know where it hurts?

PSYCHOANALYST: Let me describe a case of mine as an example. A young lady whom I'll call Carla appeared at my door, after having made an appointment, and strolled up to my desk and sat down in a very controlled, but remote way. I asked how I could help her, and she replied that she didn't know—she wasn't sure what her problem was. Then she began to talk about the things which were troubling her. She said she was depressed because she was having difficulty finding an acting job, and choosing a place to live, and deciding on an acting course. As she spoke, I gathered that she found it difficult to meet people and that she became very tense when she felt she was being judged. I said almost nothing; I simply nodded occasionally and that seemed enough to keep her talking. I certainly didn't fire a barrage of questions at her such as "Are your parents alive?" or "Are you married?" or write her answers on a form sheet.

LAWYER: Why not? Don't you have to know those things?

PSYCHOANALYST: Yes, but usually I prefer to let the patient tell me about himself in his own way; the very manner in which the vital statistics come out is often revealing. During the first interview I learned from Carla's ramblings that she came from a small New England town where her Italian family had a hardware store, that she was the youngest in a family of five girls, and the only one who didn't have to work in the store with the mother and father. I learned that they had all pampered her, wanted her to achieve things they had not, had paid for her acting lessons, and were financing her efforts to become a successful actress in New York. But along with all these data, which came out in a disorganized manner, I gleaned a good deal of emotional tone, which made it well worth the extra effort to listen and unscramble data offered in a rambling fashion.

TEACHER: Don't you ask any questions?

PSYCHOANALYST: Yes, sometimes. But I listen for clues as to *what* questions to ask. The patient gives me those clues by the order in which he tells me things, in his repetitions and hesitations, and in the pitch of his voice. I might ask a specific question when one patient mentions his brother and passes on too quickly to something else, or I might ask for more information when I perceive that another patient pauses a good deal over a description of his courting days. Sometimes there has to be a good deal of subtle prodding, especially in view of the fact that many neurotic people have a surprisingly powerful wish to present themselves as completely normal, even to the man they've come to for help. I had one man who, at his initial interview, actually forgot to tell me he was impotent with his wife—the symptom which brought him to me in the first place. On the other hand, many a woman will tell me at the first meeting the whole story of a marriage bogged down in mutual cruelties, and pour forth a wealth of intimate details while tears run freely down her cheeks. I won't have to say more than a word or two to keep her going.

But with every patient there are times when it's necessary for me to speak. Perhaps I can't hear him because he is mumbling due to a feeling of embarrassment or hostility; even though I understand his feelings, I tell him that if he wants me to hear him he will have to speak louder, so that I can examine his words as well as his attitude toward them. Again, he may make some obscure statement that I need to understand, and I must ask him for clarification. I don't try to handicap myself unnecessarily. I simply want to obtain the patient's history with all the feelings he has toward it.

LAWYER: And working in that fashion, are you able to get all the information you need in one interview, which I assume is one of your analytic fifty-minute hours?

PSYCHOANALYST: Not always. Very frequently I have to ask the patient to come back. It may take two or three interviews before I can tell whether psychoanalysis seems the proper treatment to recommend.

HOUSEWIFE: But doesn't the patient want to know what you think at the end of the first hour? What do you tell him?

PSYCHOANALYST: I say that very frankly I need more time with him to decide. I do try to offer some reassurance, if I can do so without the possibility of having to revise my opinion later. I may indicate that his problems are not strange to me, or that I am hopeful, or the like, so that he can go off at least somewhat comforted. With Carla, however, at the end of the first interview, I was able to say that I'd see what we could do together, and we agreed on a three-month trial period, and on the fee and an appointment schedule.

LAWYER: Wait a minute. No diagnosis? Don't you tell the patient what's wrong with her?

PSYCHOANALYST: No, an analyst doesn't do that. It serves no purpose. If a man is afraid he won't be able to keep from throwing a brick at someone, my telling him he's suffering from an obsessional neurosis won't help him either to control his feelings or to alter them. It would be no more useful than his wife's calling his ideas ridiculous or telling him not to worry. Indeed, pasting a psychiatric label on his symptoms may upset him unnecessarily.

LAWYER: What do you do then? Just say, "Lie down and let's get started"?

PSYCHOANALYST: There are several things I must make clear to the analysand—the patient—at the outset. First of all, he may believe that he will begin to get better right away and will continue at a steady pace. My own personal practice is to warn him that this isn't necessarily true, and that psychoanalysis is first an upsetting and *then* a restorative process. I also advise him that for the duration of the treatment he is to make no basic changes in his life without an agreement.

TEACHER: What do you consider basic?

PSYCHOANALYST: Changing jobs, for instance, or getting married or divorced, or quitting school.

TEACHER: Why do you tell him that?

PSYCHOANALYST: For one thing, many people find it less disturbing to act than to think, and may do something impulsive simply to procure relief from a passing emotion aroused in the analytic process. A more important reason, however, is that neurotic actions have produced the patient's unhappy situation. I naturally want to keep him from committing more such acts. The object of psychoanalysis, after all, is to be able to understand one's unconscious motives and drives, and control them, so that one will be able to act differently and more wisely in the future.

TEACHER: Do you give him any other instructions? Do you suggest that he read some books on psychoanalytic theory, for example?

PSYCHOANALYST: No, indeed. It isn't necessary, and for some patients it's actually quite harmful, especially in the beginning. At one point, Carla read some Freud in the hope of taunting me with what she thought might be superior knowledge, but fortunately for her own progress, she quickly discarded the project. You see, a patient may attempt to hide behind his knowledge to escape his own emotions, or may use it to impress the analyst, or argue with his interpretations, or delay coming to grips with his problems. So it turns out, ironically, that theoretical knowledge often causes treatment to proceed slower rather than faster.

HOUSEWIFE: Does the analysis go faster if, while he's home, the patient writes down things to talk about to you?

PSYCHOANALYST: It makes little difference. He can make notes at home if he wishes, providing that when he comes to the session he doesn't try to confine himself to them, but lets his mind and thoughts roam freely.

LAWYER: You've said nothing so far about the patient's family. Aren't they told anything about what's going on? Don't you have to see them to get their side of the story?

PSYCHOANALYST: The analyst is not a judge, so he doesn't have to have "their side of the story." Carla, of course, had no relatives in the city. But an early interview with the important members of the family *can* help to give a clearer picture of how much distortion there is in the patient's later presentation of events. And there are other reasons why it may be useful—though not essential, and not connected with "evidence"—to see them at least once: the analyst knows how disturbing and costly the patient's analysis is going to be for the rest of the family; he knows they will frequently feel that they are being watched and judged without knowing whether it is a fair judgment; and they will resent what they consider the patient's privilege of being able to talk it out which is denied to them. It is possible to offset all this somewhat by meeting these people early in the course of the analysis.

I had one young woman—I'll call her Ellen—who had been married six years and had three children, hated her adoring husband, and was still struggling to free herself from the emotional ties to her mother and father, who lived near her. I used to get constant phone calls, some pleading, some angry, not only from the distraught husband, but from the worried mother as well. But Ellen had to have complete confidence in my loyalty to her, and it was most important for the progress of the analysis that she have no doubt or fear that I was more concerned with her husband's or her parents' feelings. So I acted as I generally do—and as most analysts do: I had one interview, early in Ellen's treatment, with her husband. (In other cases, the interview may be with the mother or some other close relative.) I explained what he had to expect and how he ought to behave toward her, and I warned against premature reactions toward her behavior during analysis; but I did this only after I had told Ellen I wanted to do so, and got her consent, and in addition I reported the interview to her afterward.

HOUSEWIFE: How *should* the family behave?

PSYCHOANALYST: Patiently, patiently. In spite of their curiosity, they should not encourage the patient to talk about his analysis, but rather suggest that he keep his problems for the analytic session. The family will be doing the patient a great favor if they can maintain a calm, uninvolved attitude no matter how unreasonable, depressed, argumentative, or childish the patient becomes. If they can manage to act in this disinterested fashion, it will be far easier for the analysand. Outsiders—friends, relatives, or neighbors—ought to behave the same way toward the patient.

CAREER GIRL: Well, it should be a good deal easier for them. They aren't directly involved.

PSYCHOANALYST: True. Carla, who had no close relatives here, had made the acquaintance of a number of girls who were certainly kind and well-meaning. But they were interested in knowing her progress, and once one inquired at precisely the wrong moment; the question precipitated a deep-seated self-doubt, and resulted in quite a long period of depression. Naturally, this reaction can't be foreseen by either the patient or the friends. There's still another reason for a disinterested attitude. In an attempt to dissipate the painful effects of the probing going on in the analyst's office, the patient may seize the opportunity to talk to an outsider, and this slows down the analytic progress.

TEACHER: How does it do that?

PSYCHOANALYST: When Ellen, for instance—the young woman who couldn't break away from her parents—poured out her troubles to them after a disturbing session with me, she received the same enervating, relaxing sympathy she had been getting from them since she was a little girl. She felt relieved emotionally because of the cathartic effect, but this delayed her facing the nature of her excessive dependence on them. And while they were trying to make her feel better, they were being badly disturbed at finding her so upset. So it's really better for everyone if the subject is avoided.

CAREER GIRL: Psychoanalysis sounds like a pretty miserable experience, and not only for the analysand.

PSYCHOANALYST: Part of it undoubtedly is, especially because long-hidden secrets begin to come out. People usually try, for instance, to shield others as well as themselves from their neurotic traits, but analysis causes them to stop doing so. One of my patients—an engineer whom I'll call Alfred—succeeded for years in fooling his friends, family, and colleagues into thinking of him as a man of extraordinary stability and poise, happy and successful in his work. But he lived in perpetual fear of being exposed as a worthless fraud, and when he came to analysis and went through the painful and distressing experience of facing his illness, symptoms which he had never acknowledged became aggravated. His compulsive tendencies, which up to then had been channeled into productive business traits, suddenly overflowed into clearly neurotic actions. He couldn't stand to have an unanswered letter remain on his desk, and if his phone was allowed to ring more than twice, he would scream at his secretary. His sickness became so obvious that his family and friends were shocked and angry with the psychoanalyst, attributing the worsening to his influence. But, as I'll explain later, the uncovering of these symptoms was a step forward, disturbing as it may have been to Alfred and horrifying as it may have appeared to his friends.

TEACHER: How do people manage to keep their jobs in this condition? Doesn't their work suffer?

PSYCHOANALYST: No doubt it does, sometimes. But the patient's problems are usually connected with much closer relationships than business ones, however, and he can usually manage to maintain a seemingly normal attitude at his job, while he takes out his increasingly troubled feelings on his family. And once he does begin to make progress, he usually finds a great deal of extra energy released which can and does result in greater productivity.

HOUSEWIFE: It's too bad that the family must suffer.

PSYCHOANALYST: Sometimes the members of the family can successfully suggest that the patient report his home activities to the analyst. More rarely, the patient may even find it useful or necessary to live away from his family for a time. A good deal of distress may be eliminated for everyone in these ways, since on occasion the patient may inadvertently reveal hostile feelings toward his wife or family, which he is just beginning to recognize in analysis, and he may create permanent damage to the relationship even as he is ridding himself of the feelings. In addition, a separation may shorten the analytic process.

TEACHER: How does that happen?

PSYCHOANALYST: Sometimes the patient uses his family to escape from the difficulties analysis is trying to make him face. If he's discovering that he's a weak-willed, thoughtless mischief-maker, it's all too easy to have Mama say it isn't so.

HOUSEWIFE: That may explain a story I heard, which shocked me terribly. A young man I know was advised not to see his mother for a whole year during his analysis. I find that hard to take. After all, think of the mother's feelings!

PSYCHOANALYST: I'm sure she suffered, and it is certainly regrettable. But let's not assume that motherhood is always ideal; she may have been so overprotective of her son, so tenacious in her love for him, that he was never able to make a real decision for himself, and instead had developed into an insecure, impotent, emotional cripple, baffled by a world less concerned and solicitous than Mother.

LAWYER: So now instead of being dependent on Mom he'll be dependent on the analyst.

PSYCHOANALYST: Perhaps at first. But the analyst won't act as his mother does, and the analytic couch isn't his mother's bed.

TEACHER: Now we come to the heart of the matter. What happens on the couch that changes a person?

PSYCHOANALYST: You've frequently heard me mention free association as a vital factor in psychoanalysis. Now I'll try to show you how it works in practice. The analyst suggests that the patient lie down on the couch and begin to talk. He tells him he is expected to make a real effort to abandon the conscious censorship of his thoughts and to say anything which comes into his mind. If he suddenly wonders whether the analyst wears striped shorts, he should voice that wonder. If he feels that he would like to strangle his son, he should say so. If a fleeting memory of his days as a Communist recurs, he is expected to admit it.

LAWYER: But why does he have to lie on a couch?

PSYCHOANALYST: Because, as I said at our first meeting, he can usually relax more completely and let his thoughts wander with greater ease. Since he doesn't see the analyst, he is less aware of, or concerned about, the doctor's reactions and attitudes, and is freer to follow his own train of ideas without straining or censoring. All this is explained to the patient before he's asked to lie down.

HOUSEWIFE: I should think it would make some people feel more uncomfortable—perhaps even defenseless.

PSYCHOANALYST: There are people for whom it is too difficult or painful, especially in the beginning. And with these people the analyst will change the procedure. But most patients find it much easier to relax and speak freely lying down.

TEACHER: Why is it so important that the patient say anything that comes to mind?

PSYCHOANALYST: We have learned by experience that this is the way to reach a person's unconscious thoughts. The method of free association is an application of the knowledge that psychological processes can't move from one thought to another without some connection. But many of the links are unconscious.

TEACHER: If the links are unconscious, how do you find them?

PSYCHOANALYST: By studying the patient's associations. We note not only the conscious logic of a patient's communications, but the sequence in time of his ideas and feelings. And so we discover that certain ideas, feelings, and actions which happen at the same time are bound to one another in a meaningful pattern.

At one session, for instance, Alfred, the seemingly successful engineer I spoke of earlier, mentioned a news article on the sentencing of a juvenile delinquent, and as he spoke of it he felt a wave of fear come over him. He communicated that, too, and as he described this inexplicable emotion, he suddenly remembered his aunt looking at him sternly. In this case, especially since I have already picked out the salient facts for you, it is obvious that the associative pattern revealed the remnants of a childhood guilt. But in the flow of associations brought out in most cases, the unconscious connection between ideas and feelings is often very hard to ascertain; in fact, much of the psychoanalyst's work is devoted to the investigation of it.

Carla, for instance, rather early in her analysis, told me that one of her sisters, Maria, had died at the age of twelve, when Carla herself was ten. She had been completely unmoved by the funeral, she said, although she had had a number of nightmares in the years following, in which an angel that she had seen on a grave at the cemetery seemed about to strike her. It took many more months, however, before I discovered that she felt responsible for Maria's death, because, jealous of any attention the family gave to anyone else, she had often wished her dead. Thus, even though it was influenza that killed Maria, Carla still carried a burden of guilt buried in her unconscious.

LAWYER: Analysis sounds like a mystery story.

PSYCHOANALYST: And one with no easy solution. For, curiously enough, when the patient simply lies on the couch and tries to speak his thoughts, he finds himself unable to speak easily and freely. He must constantly struggle with the impulse to hold back some idea or not to talk at all, or to rearrange his words into pleasanter and more acceptable forms, so that the psychoanalyst might think well of him. Throughout the analysis, the psychoanalyst has to work at ridding his patient of inhibitions which prevent or distort his free-associating, and no analysand associates in a completely free fashion until he's close to the end of treatment.

CAREER GIRL: The idea of telling anyone some of *my* thoughts is grisly.

PSYCHOANALYST: Those shocking thoughts emerge in all sorts of ways, many of which you yourself cannot recognize as self-revelation. As, for instance, your dreams. That's why dreams are so useful to the analyst.

LAWYER: But suppose the patient doesn't dream. I know the only time I dream is when I've eaten something before I go to bed. I'd be a great subject for analysis, if I had to have indigestion in order to play ball.

PSYCHOANALYST: It only seems so to you. Physical stimuli such as an upset stomach, or noise, or hunger, or cold do make you dream, and some of them even specifically cause the *kind* of dream you have. You've probably all had the experience in which the ringing of an alarm clock has been incorporated in a dream of, say, a visitor who is persistently ringing the doorbell, until you hurry to answer it, awaken, and realize it was the clock. Internal stimuli have the same effect; going to bed hungry, for instance, may produce dreams of food-laden tables. In short, whatever the disturbance, outer or inner, the dream makes an effort to keep the sleeper from awakening; dreams are the guardians of sleep. When they are successful, the dreamer doesn't awaken.

LAWYER: I can't see how dreaming about taking Alka-Seltzer could help you.

PSYCHOANALYST: Probably not. But in addition to the physical stimuli which I just mentioned, there are psychic disturbances, and these have their effect on dreams, too. The function of the dream remains the same, you see: whether the effort is to gratify a physical desire for food or an unconscious and repressed desire for sexual relations, the dream's purpose is to fulfill the desire in one way or another, and thus to allow the dreamer to sleep on. Dreams are almost always a reflection of some conflict of which we are either unaware or reluctant to acknowledge when we're awake.

Ellen, for example, the unwilling wife, brought me a dream in which she was on an island, unable to swim and so to reach the mainland on which she saw her children playing. In life she was very confused about her feelings toward them, guilty about not loving them enough, and yet wishing they didn't exist so that she could be free of her husband. She would like her inability to love her children not to be her fault; she would like it to be beyond her power. Freud rightly called dreams the royal road to the unconscious. The interpretation of dreams leads to crucially important material that has been repressed or thrust out of awareness—material that is terribly hard to get at in other ways.

HOUSEWIFE: How does it do that? I don't understand.

PSYCHOANALYST: Let me explain the structure of a dream, as Freud described it so remarkably in his *Interpretation of Dreams*. First of all, when we speak about what a dream *means*, we are usually talking about the unconscious disturbances which threaten to waken us. There are several kinds of these. Nocturnal sensations, like indigestion, are one kind. Then there are the preoccupations of the dreamer's current, waking life—concern about an unfinished piece of work or anticipation of a longed-for trip, perhaps—which remain unconsciously active in the dreamer's mind while he sleeps. The third kind of unconscious disturbance which makes up the meaning of the dream consists of impulses which have been repressed or denied awareness in waking life, as Ellen's buried wish to be free of her children. All these unconscious disturbances—the true reason for and meaning of dreams—are known as the latent dream content, while the conscious part of the dream, the part we remember and are aware of, is known as the manifest dream content.

HOUSEWIFE: But why don't we dream what we mean? Why is everything so changed around?

PSYCHOANALYST: Let me use a metaphor. It is as though the deeply disturbing impulses, the repressed desires which are kept in the dungeon of the unconscious, can only make an appearance by disguising themselves before the jailer, the ego. Even this won't work by day, when the ego is wide-awake and alert, but at night the dungeon keeper becomes more relaxed, and then, in costume, the wish manages to sneak by. But though the ego-warden may doze, it never completely loses control. And how strong a hold it maintains determines the extent of the disguise the wish must put on to slip by, and make an appearance in the manifest dream.

Suppose a woman has a repressed wish still buried in her unconscious from her childhood for sexual relations with her father. This wish might be represented in the manifest dream by an image of the dreamer and her father fighting together with an accompanying feeling of sexual excitement. But if the ego's defenses oppose such a bald expression of this incestuous wish, the sexual excitement may be barred. If this is still too close to the original fantasy to be tolerated by the ego without anxiety or guilt, the image of the father may not appear, and instead the dreamer may be fighting with someone else, her son, perhaps. If struggling is still too close to the original impulse, it may be replaced by some other activity, as, for example, playing chess or tennis. Even this may be objectionable to the ego, and the manifest dream may be of a strange woman playing chess with the dreamer's son.

CAREER GIRL: Goodness, how devious!

PSYCHOANALYST: Yes, by the time we become adults our dream life is certainly complicated. In childhood, however, when there have not yet been many repressions, what a child wants is openly given in his dream. If a two-year-old cries for candy, and is refused, when he is put to bed he dreams contentedly that he's sucking a lollipop. But as we grow older, our lives become more sophisticated and complex. Dr. A. A. Brill, a pioneer among American psychoanalysts, described the changes well. A little boy at the zoo, four or five years old, seeing a tiger for the first time, asks if he can have one. The boy's father tells him that they can't keep him in their apartment, so the little boy dreams that he has a little tiger in a bird cage. He thinks the difficulty lies in the size of the animal, and he solves the problem very neatly in the dream. A year later this boy wants a pony, and is heartbroken that he can't have it. He dreams that he has a pony, and that it becomes lame, and he doesn't want it at all. You see how his dream indicates how much more complex life now is for him.

TEACHER: You're agreeing with Freud, then, that every dream is a wish fulfillment?

PSYCHOANALYST: Most analysts do. But even those who do not accept this point of view agree that the dream does show the nature of the analysand's conflicts, and that the detection of those unconscious struggles is of enormous value to understanding the patient.

CAREER GIRL: But I've had dreams in which I have *not* got something I've wanted. How can a dream of disappointment be a wish fulfillment?

PSYCHOANALYST: Such a dream is harder to explain, but on analysis even it, too, can usually be proven to be a fulfillment of a wish. Here's an example which Freud gives: A man had spent the night with a married woman and was afraid she might become pregnant with his child. Toward morning he dreamed that as he was about to ride off with a lovely woman, he was stopped and told he was to be arrested for infanticide. According to Freud, the dream showed how, in a highly disguised way, his fear was allayed. There was no baby in the dream, for he had done away with it, as the attempted arrest indicated. By the way, by association with the dream, the dreamer connected infanticide with birth control.

LAWYER: You may have explained that one, but I still don't understand how you can say all dreams show wish fulfillment. How about nightmares? What wish does it gratify, to be frightened out of your wits?

PSYCHOANALYST: These dreams—we call them anxiety dreams —occur when the ego-jailer falls asleep, and some repressed wish slips out of its dark cell into the light of consciousness, that is, into the manifest dream. When this forbidden impulse manages to appear in a form which is too direct or too recognizable for the ego to tolerate, the ego reacts with anxiety. You remember that this is what happens in a neurosis, in waking life: when a repression comes dangerously close to consciousness, anxiety results.

Here is a simple dream for an example: Ellen, the young married woman, dreamed she was on a sinking ship and the women and children were being sent into lifeboats. She refused to leave her husband, but suddenly she found herself in a lifeboat, watching her husband going down with the ship, and she awakened crying, seized with terror. You see how her dream fulfills her wish to be rid of her husband, but her anxiety—her nightmarish feeling—was produced by an ego outraged by the fulfillment. Of course, I couldn't be sure of this until her associations made the meaning clear.

CAREER GIRL: Then according to Freud, all anxiety dreams can be interpreted as a failure of the ego to keep a repressed wish buried?

PSYCHOANALYST: That's correct. The most common kind of anxiety dream, by the way, is of symbolic intercourse, frequently with a weapon, such as a dagger or a gun, and involving a struggle or a murder and the accompanying feelings of horror and panic. Here is such a dream one woman patient described to me: An old man came into a room where her mother and she were lying in bed. He pointed an umbrella at her mother, and the patient leaped up and made an effort to turn the umbrella away from her mother, toward herself. She described her feelings as of intense fear lest her mother or she be hurt, but she felt that she had to protect her mother from this man. Her associations confirmed the classic interpretation—that the old man was her father, and the umbrella his penis; and the dream expressed the desire to take her father's love from her mother. So once again you see how a repressed wish slipped past the ego in disguise, won momentary gratification in the dream, and yet produced such feelings of anxiety that she woke in a panic, drenched in perspiration.

LAWYER: Now we get to the point where you tell us that every snake or pole is a penis and every lake or box is a womb, and that we got all this from some primeval ancestors.

PSYCHOANALYST: There do seem to be fairly universal symbols —visual representations of objects or ideas or people—which are common to everyone. It isn't necessary, however, to become mystical about it. Since we share a common culture we're bound to have similar associations. No analyst, however, including Freud, would suggest that these universal dream symbols mean precisely the same thing to every individual. The snake you mentioned, for instance, may indeed signify a penis to a woman, but the analyst would have to know her associations with the symbol to be sure that it really had that meaning for her. For instance, to the woman who has been betrayed by a man, the snake might symbolize deceit; to the woman who, in spite of her puritanical upbringing, is nevertheless indulging in an affair with a married man, it might represent sinful desire. Again, it might not represent a penis at all; a woman who lived near a forest may have picked up a snake to show her children there was nothing to fear, and to her a snake might signify courage.

TEACHER: Well, how do you go about interpreting a dream then?

PSYCHOANALYST: By using the patient's waking associations with the symbols in his dream. We know that the manifest content is symbolic. Everything we see in the dream, every person or object, whether it's a building, a clock, a street, or a meadow, a bear, a bird, or a buffalo, represents something. And each of these symbols, human or not, may signify a person, a place, an emotion, or an abstract idea. One person may associate a certain woman whom he knows with the feeling of grief, because he remembers her weeping at a funeral. Another person may dream of a pizza and mean Pisa or Italy.

LAWYER: Is that supposed to be funny?

PSYCHOANALYST: As a matter of fact, puns are very common in

dreams. "Pizza" for "Pisa" is just one of the kinds of wit every dreamer displays—even people who are completely humorless by day. But to get back to the dream work—the way the latent content is changed into the manifest dream—there may be several meanings, condensed into one symbol. For example, the engineer, Alfred, I spoke of before, was hesitant about bringing up a certain topic during treatment, because he was afraid of my disapproval. He dreamed that he was standing at the edge of a precipice and threateningly near him was a person who reminded him of me, and also of a former employer who had been extremely harsh, and also, curiously enough, of his very severe aunt, who had actually punished him for a failing mark in high school. You might suspect, as his previous history actually confirms, that all three figures were symbols of punitive authority to him.

But there is also the opposite of condensation; there is often a reinforcement of a single meaning through repetition in different symbols. In the same dream a certain friend might be symbolized by a book which the dreamer had discussed the previous day with that friend, and by the street where the friend lives, and by another individual with some of the features of the friend.

LAWYER: And you track all this down by the patient's associations with each part of the dream?

PSYCHOANALYST: And by finding out what kind of feeling he had at the time, too. The emotions can seem quite unexpected or even contrary to the situation the patient has described, and yet they can be the clue that reveals the meaning of the dream. For example, the analyst Walter Bonime relates the following:

A young homosexual came to him saying that he had heard a great deal about him and was confident that he could help him get rid of his perversion. Very early in his treatment he reported a dream in which he was walking along a certain street and came to a group of people waiting in line for hot dogs. He looked forward eagerly to having one, but soon he realized that he was actually part of a bus queue, and he felt extremely disappointed. In discussing the dream, he associated the street with the analyst's office and the hot dog with a penis, and with the bus he had connections of getting somewhere, and thought the bus ride symbolized his analysis. He felt that the dream indicated his eagerness for treatment. The analyst, however, pointed out that his happiness had been connected with having the hot dog, while the feeling attached to the bus queue was disappointment and frustration. Therefore, the analyst suggested that though the patient said he wanted help, what he was more interested in at that point was seducing the analyst. You see how important it was to know how the dreamer felt as he experienced the dream events. Without adequate understanding of these feelings, this patient would be a potential drop-out.

TEACHER: Don't your patients sometimes describe dreams in which they feel certain emotions, but aren't themselves taking part in the dream events?

PSYCHOANALYST: Yes, but the dreamer is always in the dream, even if he is only represented symbolically. He always plays a leading part, and sometimes more than one, as when various aspects of his personality are symbolized differently. Ellen had a dream in which she was running through a garden toward a summerhouse where she saw a doll lying at the feet of a man and woman. As she ran, she kept knocking over statues which she described as mummies. In her dream, you see, she was depicted as herself, the little doll with her parents, and a mother, or "mummy." That's another example, by the way, of the play on words that goes on in the dream work.

HOUSEWIFE: Dreams seem to be so confused. Bits of only yesterday mixed up with events of long ago. Why is that?

PSYCHOANALYST: All dreams are a condensation of the past and the present. And almost every dream has more than one meaning, and represents not only some present conflict, but a similar psychological struggle from the dreamer's past as well.

HOUSEWIFE: Dream analysis certainly sounds fascinating.

PSYCHOANALYST: Much more than that. It's an extremely useful technique. The richness of the symbolism is a great help in making the patient aware of the significance and power of the precipitating emotion. A young man, who had always held himself to be kind and generous, dreamed that he was a hawk, waiting to pounce on his fiancée, and as a result it was far easier for him to recognize his cruelty than it would have been from a blunt recital of his heartless and selfish actions.

In addition, the analyst is able to mark the progress of the analysis by his patient's dreams. A patient begins analysis, half fearful of what will become of him, or of how he will be changed. Carla had a dream which showed that she was afraid of revealing herself because she was ashamed of some things in her life. She dreamed that she stood in front of a closet, which was closed. Before it stood a trunk, which she was about to unlock. She described her feelings as uneasy, and she associated the phrase "a skeleton in the closet" with the dream.

CAREER GIRL: That's certainly understandable.

PSYCHOANALYST: On the other hand, when she was close to termination of treatment, she dreamed of finding herself in a maze. This happened frequently in her dreams, but at the point I'm describing, instead of wandering helplessly about, with increasing anxiety, she simply broke through the confining walls of the maze and walked away free. Clearly, by this point she had achieved an independent, problem-solving attitude.

LAWYER: You've made the analyst appear to be a highly skilled detective, but earlier you stated that he does not judge or condemn the patient. Let me then ask you this: What does the detective-analyst do if he discovers through the patient's dreams or free associations that his patient is planning murder or suicide? Does he still preserve his nonjudging, noncondemning attitude?

PSYCHOANALYST: You're suggesting a most extreme case. If a plan like that actually approached fulfillment, and there was real danger to the patient or to some other person, the analyst would be obliged to take steps to stop him. But it is the analyst's job to divert such aggressive impulses toward himself, as the first step in helping the patient to understand and control them.

LAWYER: How does he do that?

PSYCHOANALYST: Curiously enough, he does it by *not* doing a number of things—by not directing the analysand, by not replying to his questions, by refusing to be anything but receptive and calm. This is a frustrating experience to the patient, and the analyst very quickly becomes to him the embodiment of the hated —or loved—individuals in his life.

TEACHER: Are you talking about transference?

PSYCHOANALYST: Yes, I am. I'll tell you at the next session how it is used in analysis; how, too, the patient himself struggles against being analyzed; and how the analyst, like a Horatio Alger hero, finally wins out.

CHAPTER

SEVEN

THE LONG HAUL

Transference—what it is and how it works; the honeymoon period of analysis, and when it's over; why analysis is often painful; when the analyst speaks; the strange ways of resistance; the development of insight; working through.

PSYCHOANALYST: We ended our last discussion by mentioning transference. In analysis this is the unconscious attachment to the analyst of attitudes and feelings which were originally associated with the important persons in one's early life. Transference is an inherent part of the psychoanalytic situation, but the word itself is much misunderstood. It includes all sorts of feelings the patient has toward the analyst, some of them very powerful. Because this aspect of it has been exaggerated, many people tend to think of analysts as either dreadful Svengalis or all-powerful Jupiters. Actually, a transference of emotions is made by everyone in all kinds of situations. To take very trivial examples, there is the fondness a lover feels toward a glove recently worn by his beloved, or the warm devotion a patriot feels toward his country's flag.

CAREER GIRL: I remember a movie where the heroine lovingly stroked a tube of toothpaste which had just been squeezed by the hero.

PSYCHOANALYST: And there is the horror a person feels toward the bed from which his mother's dead body has just been removed. But these are, at least to some degree, conscious emotions and actions. The neurotic's behavior and feelings are rather more under the sway of the unconscious, and his attitudes toward other people are quite frequently irrational. He unconsciously assigns motives to them that have nothing to do with the reality of who and what they are, but are carry-overs from his childhood experiences. Ellen, the young married woman I mentioned, unconsciously expected everyone she met to baby her and protect her, as her parents had done, and her charming, childlike manner did indeed inspire protective feelings in most people—at least until they began to feel put upon. Carla, the aspiring actress, antagonized almost everyone by her aloofness, and so brought about the very rejection she tried to protect herself from. In just this way, a neurotic will transfer feelings and motives from the past onto people in the present, repeating this in relationship after relationship. But when, inevitably, he or she repeats it with the analyst, there is a profound difference.

TEACHER: Is it a different kind of transference when the analyst is the object of it?

PSYCHOANALYST: No, the transference is the same, but the analyst's behavior is different. This is the very heart of the matter: he does not react as other people have. He refuses to baby someone like Ellen and he won't allow himself to take offense at the coldness of someone like Carla. Instead, the analyst studies these transferred feelings, calls them to the patient's attention, analyzes them, and traces them to their origins. Now you can see why it is so important that the analyst remain a comparatively unknown figure to the patient. When the engineer of whom I've spoken before began to talk to me in an apologetic fashion, tugging at his forelock like a small boy, I knew he had no valid reason for treating me like his stern father, and I at once felt freer to investigate his behavior.

HOUSEWIFE: Does the patient really imagine he's talking to someone else—his father, as you suggested—or does he know he's talking to the analyst?

PSYCHOANALYST: Oh, he knows he's talking to the analyst. He hasn't lost touch with reality to that extent. That would be a psychotic delusion. But he misinterprets or distorts the analyst's behavior, or has unreasonable expectations of him.

HOUSEWIFE: But is the patient necessarily unreasonable? If he's apologetic toward the analyst, isn't it possible that the analyst really *is* stern? Why must you assume that the patient is reacting to his transferred feelings toward his father?

PSYCHOANALYST: Your point is well taken. But when I speak of transference, I am referring only to those feelings towards the analyst which are *ir*rational, which are *not* warranted by him. Certainly not every thought the patient has can be the result of transference. The patient is going to have some reactions to the analyst himself, who is, after all, a human being. In the early years of psychoanalysis, if a patient told the analyst that he looked like a pig, the analyst might have been inclined to think, "Ah, he thought his father was dirty and greedy, like a swine," but today the analyst recognizes that even if the patient is transferring, there may be some reality on his side—the analyst may indeed look like a pig. And when the patient is angered by the analyst's silence, that's not an unexpected reaction, but is brought on by the analyst's carefully considered technique of frustrating him in order to elicit buried thoughts and emotions. The curious thing, however, and one which shows how the transference is working, is that the analyst's silence can be interpreted by the patient, not simply as waiting for the patient to speak, but as anger, or disgust, or amusement, or boredom. And not only does the patient think the analyst feels these emotions, but the patient himself will have all these reactions—and more—toward the analyst, as the treatment proceeds.

CAREER GIRL: Then the patient doesn't always act as though the analyst is his beloved mother?

PSYCHOANALYST: No, not exclusively. But of course it *is* true that the most important relationships in a person's life, the ones which most influenced the shaping of his character, the ones which still, though unconsciously, strongly affect his feelings and actions, *were* the early ones with members of his immediate family. And they are therefore the ones most likely to arise through free association. As a result, then, the patient will most frequently transfer to the analyst the attitudes he displayed toward these special people, of whom Mother was one of the most special.

In the course of analysis, however, he recalls a good many incidents in his life. For instance, Alfred, the engineer who had come to analysis because he was finding no satisfaction in his personal relationships, told me early in the analysis of his father's coldness, and later he described several of his teachers and even his employer as having the same repelling aloofness. Then he told me that I, too, was cold, reserved, and unfriendly. He also described with great agitation and red-faced confusion a childhood sweetheart who was very different—warm and affectionate and sexually exciting. But he felt overwhelmed with guilt about her and was ashamed of what his father would think of the son's passionate responses to her affection. This, too, was reflected in the analytic situation, and the patient grew angry at me for encouraging such forbidden feelings. Again, there was his aunt, the family tyrant, whose opinions and authority were feared by everyone; I became that figure to him, too, at times, and he would tell me that he was afraid—though it seemed irrational to him as he said it—that I would punish him for his wrong ideas.

HOUSEWIFE: Do all these transferences flit by rapidly or does the patient spend months treating the analyst as he treated his father, acting sullen and scared all during that time, and then spend months more loving the analyst as he did his mother?

PSYCHOANALYST: His feelings are not all that clear-cut. As in life, the analysand's feelings toward the analyst are mixed; hate and love are always present, though one may be visible more often than the other. However, in most analyses the analyst and the patient tend to spend quite a long time exploring each important relationship in the patient's life, and during the period when the subject of the father, for example, comes up again and again, the analysand rather consistently will act as if the analyst were his father and actively relive the emotions of the recalled events with the analyst-father.

But this is only part of the analytic process. I think it might help if I return to a specific case and show you how it works in a given instance. You remember that when Carla, the actress, came to me, she behaved in a cold, seemingly self-assured, aloof manner, which she had adopted to protect herself from the rebuffs she feared from everyone. She wanted to be loved, but she was afraid to offer affection, because of her expectation of a hostile response. She was unable even to return affectionate overtures; she couldn't believe in their sincerity or their duration. She insisted on paying me in advance—out of fear of spending the money elsewhere, she mistakenly claimed—in the hope of thus assuring my attention and affection. She complained of long, frightening depressions, when she was unable to do any of the things she had to do, such as look for a part in a play, or go to acting class, or find an apartment. In her controlled, completely unemotional manner, she described her autocratic father, and the way he alternated unreasonable strictness with doting fondness; her too busy mother, who left Carla in the care of her sisters; and the responsibility she felt to all of them for having worked long, hard hours in the store to pay for all her singing, dancing, and dramatic lessons. She related that in acting class she was so concerned about how she appeared to the other participants that she couldn't concentrate on her dramatic interpretation. Trying out for a part in a professional play was still worse, and sent her into a state of near-panic.

LAWYER: What, no sexual problem?

PSYCHOANALYST: You'll be pleased to know that she did have a sexual problem. She feared and hated sex, although she had no firsthand knowledge of the act of intercourse. She didn't want to be a woman at all; every month, in fact, she would suffer severe menstrual cramps and bemoan her fate in being female.

CAREER GIRL: Was it difficult for her to tell you all this?

PSYCHOANALYST: No, it was easy. It usually is, at the beginning. And for the first few months simply telling me her troubles made her feel less anxious. In spite of the aloofness which was evident at the beginning of each session, she was grateful and friendly to me, and felt better and more optimistic generally. This early time of optimism is often known as the "honeymoon period." The first cathartic effects of the patient's spilling out his troubles make him feel he has found an all-powerful father, one who will cure him by magic, and he is sure that everything is going to be lovely.

TEACHER: And when is the honeymoon over?

PSYCHOANALYST: When the patient begins to resent the analyst's inactivity. He begins to feel that he has done what the analyst asked of him; surely by now the analyst must have come to some conclusion and should be able to report it to him; the analyst should do *something* in return for his continuing cooperation—and his money. Gradually a number of vague desires and expectations, of which he wasn't aware when he began treatment, come into his mind, and he awaits their gratification by the analyst. He may think the analyst is going to find him a job, or give him specific advice and thus solve his problems for him, or even make him perfect by a kind of osmosis. But slowly he realizes that the analyst doesn't have a magic wand, and what's more has no intention of granting his wishes. He realizes that the analyst is simply sitting there listening to him and that nothing marvelous has happened to him at all; and slowly he begins to feel resentful of this obstinate man who does nothing except collect his fee at the stipulated intervals.

Of course, all this is the patient's version of the process. The analyst has spoken very little, it is true; he has used only whatever inconspicuous phrases were necessary to keep the patient's thoughts flowing, while he has been trying to discover the unconscious pattern which underlies them. But the analysand, wanting so much more, feels only a seemingly unreasonable, yet highly predictable dissatisfaction. He is afraid to tell the analyst, however, how disappointed he has become in him. He holds back, partly out of politeness, partly because he retains the hope that the analyst will do something for him, and partly because he has no one else to turn to. Meanwhile, the anger and resentment build up inside him.

TEACHER: How do you know that this is the way he feels?

PSYCHOANALYST: There are many signs visible to the trained eye. His dreams, for instance, are often the giveaway. At this point, for example, Carla had a dream of wanting to take a train to go to a particular place. She went to the railroad station and asked the ticket seller if the train went to her destination. The man didn't answer her at all, and so she didn't know if she wanted to pay him. In her dream she said she studied him carefully and then decided he didn't look like the kind of man who could be trusted with money.

TEACHER: Did Carla think that you were that man?

PSYCHOANALYST: No, but as I continued to ask questions about her associations to the dream, she suddenly burst into a tirade against me. She said that I was a fraud and that I only wanted to manipulate her and that I was no good to her at all. She went on for quite a while, but having released her feelings of anger, and having received no punishment for it, she felt better and was able to proceed more freely in telling me the things she was concerned with.

CAREER GIRL: But you'd know even without a dream, wouldn't

you, if the patient was feeling disappointment in you?

PSYCHOANALYST: Of course. Alfred showed how he felt in a typical way. He asked me, in a very roundabout fashion, what my qualifications as an analyst were.

LAWYER: And what did you tell him?

PSYCHOANALYST: I didn't tell him my qualifications. After all, he could always ascertain them in any of the ways I've already discussed with you. Instead, I asked him *why* he wanted to know, and kept after that salient point. He finally admitted that he thought I was a charlatan because I wasn't making him well more quickly. And for him, as for everyone, it was an important step in the healing process to learn that he could criticize *me*, whom he already thought of as a father, without retribution.

TEACHER: Then the patient had already transferred to you his feelings for his father?

PSYCHOANALYST: Yes. This happens with every patient. It's part of the reason for the patient's grandiose expectations of the analyst, as well as the bond that holds the patient to the analyst when those expectations are not realized.

LAWYER: But when does the patient fall in love with the analyst?

PSYCHOANALYST: That unfortunate phrase describes a very useful phenomenon, which is an extension of the patient's early expectations that the analyst will help him get a job or will find a magic solution to his problems. What happens is something like this: The patient comes to analysis wanting the analyst to cure him of his illness. But as the analysis progresses, and his overt wish is not gratified, other desires turn up, one by one. He finds he wants praise, acceptance, sympathy, and finally he recognizes in himself the most basic and universal human need of all, the one which all human beings have—the need to love and to be loved. Especially is this true as the patient uncovers and relives his childhood experiences. The original desire for the love of the parent, no matter how mixed with the resentment and fear and even hatred that the patient once felt for his mother or father, is transformed into a love of the analyst and a desire for his love. This basic need lasts until the patient learns how to find fulfillment in the outside world. And the existence of this transference love sustains the patient during the periods when he feels that analysis is bringing him nothing but pain and frustration.

HOUSEWIFE: Must he feel such pain? Can't you comfort him?

PSYCHOANALYST: He *is* comforted, enormously, by this unconsciously aroused love for the analyst. And the analyst augments this feeling by his complete acceptance of the analysand. However, the patient must be in enough pain to go on, and not rest content with this artificial relationship. The analyst, therefore, aggravates the suffering of the patient deliberately—but judiciously—by his silences and by his frequent refusal to offer guidance or advice.

TEACHER: Why is the pain necessary?

PSYCHOANALYST: For one thing, to offset the aspect of the patient's illness which is giving him solace. Alfred, for example, who had no satisfactory relationships, was nevertheless a very successful man because he drove himself compulsively. Ellen enjoyed tremendously the pity and concern her woes elicited from her parents. And Carla received a vengeful pleasure from spurning the attentions of friendly boys. Too, the frustration the patient feels because of the analyst's deliberate "inactivity" forces him to overcome the hesitation or embarrassment he feels at saying what's on his mind. No one wants to reveal that he masturbates, or that he can't achieve an orgasm with an attractive woman, or that he dislikes his children. But the most important reason for not fulfilling the patient's cravings is to force him to search further and further into his mind, stripping off layer by layer the veils which cover the old, ugly memories, until he reaches the important sources of his difficulties.

HOUSEWIFE: How do you know when the patient is revealing the important things? How do you even know which are the important things?

PSYCHOANALYST: Everything the patient says is part of a pattern which reveals his attitude toward life, and therefore his problems. In the average productive session, the patient usually touches five different areas: his dreams, his relationship with the analyst, his present or recently past life, his childhood, and sex. For example: during one session Carla demanded that I change her hours, and felt mistreated because I couldn't; she reported a dream in which she cried over a broken doll, and in her associations to the doll she said it was like an unbroken one which had belonged to her sister Maria (the one who died, you remember), and that as a child she had sulked until she was given an even larger doll of her own; she added that her sisters always gave her anything she wanted, lest she sulk; she then complained of how she had been ignored by a director when she went to try out for a new play; and she pointed out that men in general abuse women, who get nothing out of sex themselves but must submit for the sake of male pleasure. But throughout all these topics you can see one theme clearly—her desire to continue to be spoiled and pampered as she had been as a child.

TEACHER: You say that all this is what happens at a productive session. What if it doesn't? Is the session wasted?

PSYCHOANALYST: As I think I indicated before, omissions themselves are significant. If an area is consistently ignored, I raise the question of its exclusion. Some patients may fail to remember a whole period of their lives, for instance, because of a traumatic experience connected with that time. For the first several months of her analysis, Carla never mentioned her sister Maria, although she talked about the rest of the family, and I knew how many sisters she had. I finally asked her about it, and then she told me of Maria's death, from influenza, when they were both children.

LAWYER: What if there are silences, long silences, rather than omissions?

PSYCHOANALYST: When that happens, and it does frequently, I usually ask him why he isn't talking. I may have to ask him a pointed question to get him to speak. Often he'll come in so depressed or so furious that he just lies down on the couch without a word, and will continue, if not prodded, to do so day after day. Some analysts will let whole sessions go by without a word spoken, but I usually say something after ten or fifteen minutes to draw out the patient's thoughts.

But let me get back to Carla and the way her case progressed. I said, you remember, that the patient will have the same feelings toward me that he has toward other people. His behavior in my office is an intensified, highly emotionalized reflection of his behavior outside the office, and therefore of his neurosis. Carla's expectations of me, then, were those that she had of everyone. For example, she had told me of an incident in her adolescence, when her oldest sister finally rebelled against their tyrannical father and, being twenty-one, packed her bags and prepared to leave home. Her father was furious, of course, but finally, as her sister was walking out the door, he offered her some money. Her sister angrily refused it, and left. At that point Carla, unconsciously trying to show him that she wanted his love, said to her father, "If she won't take it, Papa, I will." He turned on her in a rage and said, "Drop dead."

When Carla told me this story, I privately predicted that at some time in analysis she would act toward me as she had acted toward everyone ever since that terrible scene. Though she would love me as she did her father, she would reject me, lest I reject her. And that's just what she did, in one way after another. Even her dreams reflected the struggle between distrust and a growing affection. While she was still at the stage where she was finding it extremely difficult to reveal her inner feelings, which meant to put herself in my hands, she had a nightmare in which she dreamed that she jumped from a cliff—her associations revealed that she felt she was leaping into an intimate relationship—at the urging of a "friend" who had given her a parachute. But the friend, whom she had trusted, had sealed the parachute closed, and she fell to the ground with a horrible impact.

TEACHER: Did her dreams change as time went on?

PSYCHOANALYST: Yes, as we made more progress, Carla's dreams reflected it. She reported, though it was terribly difficult for her to do so, that she had a dream in which I embraced her. She said she had a number of conflicting feelings in the dream; of well-being, of fright, and of confusion as to what the gesture meant to me.

CAREER GIRL: How did she act in the office?

PSYCHOANALYST: In the same contradictory way. Sometimes she was seductive, sometimes she was aloof. She might snap at me and then turn sweet, or she might be pleasant and then suddenly become frigid. One time she called and had me arrange, at considerable difficulty, a special appointment with her which she insisted she had to have. The following morning she had a friend call and cancel it.

HOUSEWIFE: Didn't she understand what she was doing?

PSYCHOANALYST: Only when I pointed it out to her.

LAWYER: Ah, then you don't just listen to the patient or ask an occasional question?

PSYCHOANALYST: Of course not. After the first month or so of the analysis I'm able to draw some conclusions, and I begin to make comments on the patient's statements. For instance, Carla came in one day, glared at me, and told me to straighten my tie, because she wanted *her* analyst to be well groomed. Then she lay down, sighed, and said she wished she were someone else, someone who could have everything under control. During the same session, when my phone rang, she demanded that I let it ring. I replied that she was trying to manage me. And as the session progressed, it was clear that whether she was remembering an incident in her past or reacting to her job in a producer's office, she was showing her desire to direct and control people. So in the last ten minutes or so of the session I pointed this out to her.

It's a common practice to sum up the theme of the analytic hour, although not all analysts make their comments in this fashion. Some may remind their patients from time to time of statements they had forgotten and contradicted; others may point out obvious omissions in the analysands' stories. They may do this very rarely or at almost every session, as soon as a point becomes clear to them and they feel it can be gotten across to their patients.

TEACHER: How does the patient react to what you say?

PSYCHOANALYST: In various ways. Sometimes with shock. Sometimes he refuses to accept the interpretation. Sometimes he feels the intellectual thrill of acquiring new knowledge of himself. But the most successful reaction is an emotional one. When Carla would suddenly resume her aloof, withdrawn manner with me, I would point out what she was doing, and we would discuss it. On one occasion I told her that she seemed to be trying to protect us from each other. At first she was confused by that, but after talking about it for a while she became angry, and she shouted at me. Then, her rage having been released, she suddenly felt a great surge of tenderness toward me—of friendliness and warmth and affection. Her inner feelings toward me had come to the surface. For a while she was happy and elated, and showed more cooperation in our analytic sessions.

CAREER GIRL: But she was always *trying* to be cooperative, wasn't she?

PSYCHOANALYST: Yes, of course. But this is the hard fact of the necessary length of psychoanalysis. No matter how much the patient wishes to cooperate, no matter how conscientiously he has reported the way he feels and the shameful thoughts he has, there are attitudes as well as silences which he cannot control. These obstacles to analysis, these resistances, are the forces which once buried a thought or desire, and now unconsciously continue to try to keep it buried. The neurotic habits of behavior, formed to protect the patient from pain and anxiety, continue to do their job.

The pain Carla had felt as a result of her father's rejection forced her into a hostility and distrust toward all men. She fought —unconsciously—against any warm feelings she felt, not only toward me but toward any man she knew. To her ego, such warm feelings signaled danger—a danger of being rejected. Thus, unconsciously, she continued to resist the impulse which might expose her to distress. She did this by avoiding the effects of my interpretations, when she felt threatened; whenever she felt loving feelings toward me developing, she would miss an appointment, or have to go out of town for some reason, or even try to find an excuse to drop analysis altogether.

TEACHER: Do many patients have these reactions to the discoveries they are making about themselves?

PSYCHOANALYST: Very many. When the analysis is proceeding well enough for the repressed desires and thoughts to approach consciousness, the patient almost always becomes anxious. And the analytic process sometimes brings such pain at this stage that many patients can't stand it, and run away from it in various ways. Fortunately, the anxiety the analysand experiences is offset by the feeling of need for the analyst—that basic emotion my legal friend here refers to as being "in love." Too, along with the pain goes the relief which comes when the repressed impulses are actually uncovered. You cannot overestimate the delight and freedom the patient experiences when he has exhumed a buried feeling of guilt or hatred, and gotten rid of it. He looks about him with a fresh eye; he sees new friendliness in people's faces, senses new possibilities in his formerly boring work, feels new springs of love in himself. And even if these positive feelings are only glimpses of the future, the vision of them supports him in the unpleasant times. And by this support, as well as by the love and dependence the patient continues to feel for the analyst, he is helped to overcome his resistances.

TEACHER: How does he manage to do that when he isn't even aware of them?

PSYCHOANALYST: Ah, here is where the seemingly uncooperative analyst helps, by interpreting the patient's actions and words. Once a resistant act or statement has been revealed, either by the help of the analyst's frustrating silence, or judicious questioning, or careful comment, the analyst points it out and tries to show the patient the meaning of his actions. Whenever a resistance can be shown in the form of the patient's silence, or his hostility, or by his missing an appointment, or by a dream, it's a small step forward. Pointing resistances out, examining them, analyzing them, and resolving them is at the very heart of the psychoanalytic technique.

CAREER GIRL: And you say even your dreams reveal your resistances?

PSYCHOANALYST: Very clearly. Carla described one dream in which she was hiding behind a wall because, when she walked in front of it, a photographer would take her picture. The fear that this might happen filled her with panic, she said. By her associations, it was evident that the photographer represented the analyst to her. Again, another patient, further along in analysis, and beginning to recognize the change in herself, told me of a dream in which she was taking some kind of growth pill, and was feeling very anxious lest the growth could not be halted, because a growth that couldn't be stopped was like a cancer. No patient willingly gives up his neurosis, you see.

CAREER GIRL: But you ferret it out of all its hiding places, like some hound-dog following a scent through the swamps.

PSYCHOANALYST: That sounds like one of my patient's dreams. But I must go on observing and analyzing the patient's resistances, to help him get better. And he fights me every inch of the way. He keeps producing his resistances, one after the other, tirelessly, ingeniously, stubbornly. One patient may come late, and we have to discuss his tardiness. Another may light a cigarette, although he has been told that smoking during the analytic hour is a way of avoiding some feeling or thought; then I must ask him why he lit a cigarette. Many a patient will dissipate the effect of the analytic relationship by pouring out the contents of a session to some sympathetic outsider; when I discover the "leakage," I have to remind him that he is only impeding his progress.

TEACHER: Then a patient can be resisting analysis even when he's not on the couch.

PSYCHOANALYST: Indeed he can. The unconscious ways we protect ourselves from the possibility of pain or exposure seem almost endless. Brand-new symptoms, spawned by the same old neuroses, pop up continuously. Phobias, fears of getting on an elevator to come to my office, for instance; or psychosomatic ailments, such as headaches or nausea; or compulsions, such as checking to see if all the doors are locked—these may appear in patients who had only a general feeling of anxiety when they first undertook analysis.

TEACHER: Why should a symptom appear as a means of resisting analysis?

PSYCHOANALYST: Don't you remember that a neurotic symptom is formed to relieve anxiety? Whenever a repressed throught approaches consciousness, the individual becomes anxious. It is as if the patient were in a dentist's office; when the analytic drilling exposes the raw nerve of the buried impulse, pain causes the patient's head to jerk away, or his tongue instinctively to cover the bared spot. A phobia, or some other symptom, offers the same cover during analysis that it does at any other time, so when an analysand feels the pain of anxiety, he may easily develop a new symptom. And because it does relieve the pressure, it hinders analytic progress.

CAREER GIRL: Did Carla develop symptoms, too?

PSYCHOANALYST: Yes, she did. Over the years I was treating her, she developed a rash, leg cramps, and mouth ulcers. As the anxiety which produced a symptom was examined and understood, the symptom would disappear, but when the going became rough again, another one appeared.

CAREER GIRL: No wonder analysands look so miserable sometimes, with all those busy little resistances dodging about. I suppose I'll have to be more understanding when my in-analysis friends are "acting out."

HOUSEWIFE: What do you mean? What's "acting out"?

CAREER GIRL: I mean behaving like spoiled children. Because some of them certainly do!

PSYCHOANALYST: What you're talking about is actually another form of resistance, one which often occurs outside of the analyst's office. Acting out happens when the patient behaves the way he feels, instead of identifying the feeling, remembering its origin, putting it into words, and thus grasping its significance. For example, Ellen one day simply took a book, went into her room and locked the door, and stayed there the whole day reading, ignoring the fact that her children hadn't been fed or that she hadn't eaten. She was acting as she used to when she was a little girl and didn't get her way—she would lock the door of her bedroom and read while she listened with smug satisfaction to her parents' pleading with her on the other side of the door. Acting out is another effective kind of resistance for the patient, because it offers some discharge of tension; it is a substitute for remembering.

CAREER GIRL: If it's a resistance, you can't approve of it. But I thought analysts sanctioned such behavior because it showed that the patient was overcoming his inhibitions and doing what he should have done long ago.

PSYCHOANALYST: You're mistaken, however. The analyst certainly does not approve of acting out, even if it occurs in his office. One day Carla became angry with me and instead of telling me how she felt, she flounced out of the room and slammed the door behind her. When she came for her next appointment, I asked her why she acted in this fashion and reminded her that in analysis the agreement between patient and analyst is to deal in words. She began to talk about it, and soon revealed that that was how she always got her way when she lived at home.

Curiously enough, this kind of unconscious resistance can come even when the patient has been making progress and is in a cheerful frame of mind about the analyst. One patient came into my office one day and curled up on the couch like a baby still in the womb. Then he lay there contentedly, with a happy smile on his lips but no words issuing from his mouth. Since progress is

rarely apt to be made by the patient's acting as if he were returning to the womb, I kept probing the reasons for this infantile
behavior. When the patient does his acting out in my office, you
see, I understand what he's doing and I can get him to describe
the way he feels instead of dramatizing it. And in that way, as
well as by the constant discussion of my interpretations, the patient develops insight into his behavior.

TEACHER: What do you mean by insight? You make it sound
like more than just understanding the meaning of an action.

PSYCHOANALYST: When analysts speak of insight, they mean
the emotional recognition by the patient that what he feels and
the way he acts toward other people are part of a pattern which
originated long ago and which manifests itself throughout his
life. Alfred, who as a child felt guilty at the exciting touch of a
little affectionate girl, was compelled ever after to withdraw from
a relationship with a warm, inviting woman, and to thrust himself
into the business of seeking success at his work. For him, insight
meant that he saw that the pattern of his behavior originated for a
reason which was valid at the time—his father and aunt patently
disapproved of the girl—but that the pattern persisted despite
changes in Alfred's circumstances, and that it was offensive and
injurious to other people as well as troublesome to him. Although
Alfred had been able to have intercourse with women, he never
felt warm feelings of attachment to his bed partner, and he remained emotionally inviolate. He politely but firmly rebuffed the
love which charming women offered him, and felt frozen and
loveless. He was able neither to give nor to receive the affection
he so desperately wanted in his conscious mind.

HOUSEWIFE: And telling him what was wrong with him
wouldn't have helped, wouldn't have given him insight?

PSYCHOANALYST: In the early days of psychoanalysis it was
thought that merely having the analyst explain the reason for the
patient's action would solve everything; the patient would cry
"Aha!" and understand. Unfortunately, as we have learned over
the years, intellectual acceptance is not enough. There has to be
an emotional, an unconscious, acceptance as well.

TEACHER: How do you know when that has come?

PSYCHOANALYST: It's a slow thing. First, we recognize that it is a sign of insight when the patient substantiates the analyst's suggestions. For instance, Carla tended to withdraw from unpleasant situations. When a boyfriend said something she didn't like, she hung up the phone. She stopped seeing several of her girl friends because she felt they were deliberately taking advantage of her. She didn't reply to letters from home when she felt they hadn't paid enough attention to her on her visits. If her acting teacher was critical of her, she walked out of class.

When I first pointed out that she consistently acted this way, that this was the way she expressed her anger, her aggressions, she was shocked. But she agreed. She comprehended the significance of what I said. And she proved that she had gained an insight into this aspect of her behavior by adding that that was how she used to act when she was a child. She could recall distinctly her habit of leaving the table when someone in the family said something to her which displeased her. You remember that she was the youngest child, and would have felt guilty about speaking up when one of her older sisters or a parent was being unfair. She found, instead, what was for that situation a highly satisfactory mode of behavior.

HOUSEWIFE: Well, once she had gained this insight, did she change? Did Carla stop withdrawing when she understood what she was doing?

PSYCHOANALYST: No, not at once. Indeed, it was a good deal later. Carla's response to life's situations was too ingrained, too unconsciously driven, to be changed at once. No, at another session soon after, she reacted to me in the same way, and I pointed it out to her again, and again she saw what she was doing. But unconsciously she isolated one event from the next, and saw no connection until I showed it to her. I had to link her stony silences in my office to her going off to the ladies' room when her boss gave her too much work, as well as to an old childhood memory of standing in the rain in the back yard waiting until her sister called her in and offered her the doll she had earlier refused her. And I had to do this time after time after time, throwing a spotlight on each new incident as it presented itself, saying more and more about the nature of the pattern, until, very gradually, her understanding seeped into her unconscious, and dissolved the bonds which kept her loving feelings imprisoned; and her true warmth and wish for affection became free to assert themselves. This is what is known as "working through."

TEACHER: When did the change show itself? And in what way?

PSYCHOANALYST: From the time of her first insight, she had to spend about six months "working through" the problem of her withdrawing. The change showed up in my office first, as changes always do. She became warm and friendly and obliging. And about three months later—this is average, too—her descriptions of her activities and her reactions indicated that her relationships to the rest of the world had altered as well. She reported a number of successful dates, less friction with her employer, and a more relaxed attitude regarding affairs at home.

You must realize, however, that I'm speaking of only one aspect of her behavior. She had other problems which had to be worked through in the same way: her guilt over her sister's death; her immobilizing resentment toward her family because of her feeling that she had to succeed in return for their lifelong financial support; her hatred of being a woman, having come from a home where her mother proclaimed womanhood a curse, and where sex was a dark and forbidden mystery; and her desire for control, to combat the insecurity she felt as the youngest in a large family. All these were problems which we were able to solve, although it took over five years.

Little by little, she uncovered the childhood attitudes and re-called into consciousness the once injurious experiences or patterns. Where these patterns could not be directly uncovered, we reconstructed the past by using her present actions as indications; this sparked memories in her, and she relived all those long-re-pressed emotions with me, but in a more healthful way, since she was never able to provoke the customary responses. Her fury couldn't make me respond in an angry way, her complaining elicited no contempt, and her wheedling and flirting had no effect. She saw that I was not to be manipulated, or made to play any of the roles she assigned me. I pointed out over and over that she was trying to get me to reject her or punish her or use her, and showed how she was doing this. I stated clearly just what damage she was doing to herself by thus repeating harmful and irrational behavior. And eventually she saw that loving someone was not really perilous. She did learn to love—she's now happily married, and fond of, but not dependent on, her family back in New England.

CAREER GIRL: What a success story! Human Being Makes Good!

PSYCHOANALYST: Yes, Carla's analysis would be considered a successful one. And although an analyst correctly hesitates to speak of any individual patient as typical, I can say that she represents, by the successful outcome of her case, the happy majority of analysands.

CHAPTER
EIGHT

IS IT EVER OVER?

*The analyst's goals and his criteria for termination; endless
cases and unsuccessful ones; the average length of treatment;
the meaning of improvement; how many are successful.*

TEACHER: Your description of Carla's treatment and recovery
was certainly edifying. Hers was a rather complicated case, however—or so it seemed to me. I'd like to have a better idea of when
you consider a case successful and why. I wish you'd point out
the general goals you have for all patients—even those who come
to you for help with, say, a simple phobia.

PSYCHOANALYST: First of all, let me say that people rarely
come to analysis any more with such clear-cut, uncomplicated,
single symptoms as claustrophobia or a hand-washing complex.
Perhaps today's chaotic world produces more complex problems.
Or perhaps we've become familiar enough with the psychological
processes to discern more easily the intricacy of the design. But
whatever the reason, the complaints which bring the patient to
the doctor today are usually diffuse, complicated, and unclear.
This is the reason why, at present, most analysts prefer to describe neurotic illness in terms of a whole series of actions and
reactions: a sense of alienation; an inability to express love, or to
receive affection, or to offer criticism; an unwillingness to accept
responsibility or to complete a job; feelings of unjustified anguish
or rage; and the like.

LAWYER: Have you broader goals, then, to cover these modern complaints?

PSYCHOANALYST: We hope to bring about basic character

changes that will make the analysand a mature individual, capable of dealing adequately with the outer world and with the inner man as well. We hope to make him a responsible social creature, able to satisfy his instinctual sexual strivings, but recognizing that the sexual act is only part of a much greater emotional involvement. We hope he will grow up enough to be immunized against a recurrence of his neurosis in the face of future stress. We hope he will be able to form better relationships with other people, to feel more comfortable with himself, to be more productive in his work, and to more fully and freely enjoy his leisure time.

HOUSEWIFE: Just as an example, what were your goals for Ellen, the young woman with three children?

PSYCHOANALYST: Ellen, you remember, originally hoped I would advise her to leave her husband, but *I* hoped to see her eventually able to *feel* a genuine love for him and for her children as well, to be honestly interested in what they said and thought and felt, and to be willing to admit occasional irritation without guiltily trying to find a scapegoat. I hoped that she would learn to appreciate and return the adult love of a grown man, instead of expecting to be babied by him, and resenting her children because they seemed her rivals for his attention.

HOUSEWIFE: What results did you expect in her attitude toward her parents?

PSYCHOANALYST: I hoped she would be able to move a discreet emotional distance away from her mother and father, so that she would no longer be playing in a doll's house from which she could flee when she grew tired and cross, to the arms of her waiting parents. And I hoped she would be able to do this without bitterness or hatred toward her parents, but with a greater appreciation of their goodness and greater understanding of their weaknesses. Ideally a successful analysis would give her the power to do her housework, enjoying its stimulating aspects and enduring the duller chores without feeling martyred. It would, furthermore, enable her to take pleasure in having dinner out, or indulging in an expensive hat, or luxuriating in an evening of reading in bed, without feeling either vengeful or guilty. But most important, once she grew up through analysis, she would no longer have to feed on other people's love, always demanding without giving, never sated or secure. I hoped that in analysis she would learn how to partake of love, would discover the joy of shared devotion, of unselfish affection, and of freely offered tenderness—the simple, basic delights which all people can find in each other, but, which, alas, they so rarely do.

CAREER GIRL: What lovely goals! But how about the sordid side? Don't your expectations ever include painful changes in the patient's situation, like breaking up the marriage or losing all one's old friends?

PSYCHOANALYST: It isn't part of the analyst's purpose to make fundamental changes in the life situation of every patient. The analyst finds it more realistic to help him seek emotional health within the framework of the life he's living, to help him exploit all the dormant potentialities of the situation he is in. But sometimes, if his life has been built under neurotic influences, only a radical alteration may make emotional health possible. So there *are* some situations in which the analysis becomes a surgeon's knife, providing the analysand with a tool to cut out the cancer which is feeding on the healthy tissues.

Ellen was lucky: her marriage was basically a good one. Her husband was a stable person who wanted her to grow up and be a woman rather than a child-wife. Ellen's problem was to achieve emotional independence from her parents; and since she was already separated physically from them, no overt, painful change was necessary. Had her husband, however, been a man who fed on her need to be babied, and had he been unable to allow her to grow up, the maturity which analysis produced in her would only have altered their marital difficulties. Her new maturity, however, might have forced him to seek help for himself; and at least Ellen would have had the ability to make a rational decision about *her* future. But fortunately, although she resented her husband in the beginning because he treated her as a woman, at the end his attitude helped the relationship blossom.

CAREER GIRL: And so another neurosis bites the dust! But was Ellen satisfied? She didn't seem to have your high-sounding goals to begin with.

PSYCHOANALYST: True enough. But patients rarely do. They come to analysis wanting to get rid of the pain. And in the process of emotional re-education, they do. Everything else is a bonus.

TEACHER: How do you decide when the patient has been

sufficiently "re-educated"? You obviously don't have the simple tests of a regular educational institution.

PSYCHOANALYST: That's so. But we do have a set of criteria. One way we judge is by observing the patient's self-awareness both of the changes in him and of the weaknesses which remain. He should be more realistically self-confident, and at the same time more realistically aware of his limitations. If he attempts to deny the changes or to exaggerate them, he isn't ready to deal with the world. Alfred, who had trouble relating to people, began in his second year in analysis to take out a girl rather steadily. They clearly enjoyed each other's company, and he reported many a pleasant evening of good talk and evident physical signs of affection on his part. But though his actions indicated a steady growth of maturity, he was very confused about their meaning. He couldn't believe what was happening to him. He was constantly probing himself mentally—asking himself how he felt, whether he really felt anything, and frequently insisting he felt nothing at all. While it was obvious, then, that his case was progressing, he was by no means recovered.

Toward the end of his analysis, on the other hand, when he acted in a mature way, he knew it. He told me of an incident in his office, for instance. His secretary had been so busy that she had neglected to confirm an appointment for him, and it had been canceled. Instead of being furious and upset, as once he would have been, he calmly arranged for another one, and then called his girl and took her out for a drink in the unexpectedly free hour he had. He reported the incident to me elatedly, fully understanding how different it was from earlier events in his life, and how indicative of his new spontaneity and flexibility. Further, he was confident that he would be able to react in this way in the future, and when such confidence is realistic, it, too, is an important sign of emotional re-education.

TEACHER: You said at our last meeting that the patient shows improvement first in the analyst's office. Yet the events you've described took place outside. How does the patient act with you when he's ready to discontinue analysis?

PSYCHOANALYST: He becomes more and more independent of me. He cooperates willingly and easily, of course, free-associates with no trouble, and works actively at the exploration of his own feelings and the interpretation and understanding of his dreams. He is responsive to my interpretations, but has his own opinions. He does not passively offer me his problems, but joins and even leads a discussion of them. When the analytic process was in mid-course, he felt in great need of me, and he came as a child to a parent, unable and unwilling to be a separate individual. But as he matured he discovered himself to be an entity again. He continues to enjoy my acceptance of him, and reaches for my approval, but he begins to think of me as a real person, and his own decisions become of greater importance to him. He feels that he is going through a kind of rebirth. Alfred, for instance, actually dreamed of this as he approached termination. In his dream, he said, he was in a coffin, being carried along in a funeral procession, surrounded by weeping relatives. But he knew he wasn't dead; he felt he had come to life again; and he lay in his coffin, happy and expectant, waiting for the moment to surprise and delight the people around him.

CAREER GIRL: Was it significant that you weren't in the dream?

PSYCHOANALYST: Good! You've spotted an important characteristic. Yes, I begin to fade out of my patients' dreams at this point. People consistently dream of new things—a new job, a new building, a larger, roomier apartment, and so forth. Their dreams are clearer, less confused and less masked. In short, even their unconscious tells me they're through with me.

HOUSEWIFE: What do you do when you see the patient has attained the goals you've hoped he would reach? Do you serve notice that the analysis is over or do you wait for him to leave?

PSYCHOANALYST: First, let me admit that I've described the ideal situation, in which both the analyst and the patient are satisfied. More often, the patient wants to leave although the analyst is aware of attitudes still to be changed and lessons yet to be learned. But if the patient's desires are reasonable, and his practical needs have been met by the treatment, the analyst will very likely agree that the analysis can be successfully terminated. Therefore, when the patient asks again about ending the analysis —he does this quite often in the course of treatment—at a time when signs of improvement have become evident, I agree with him as to the possibility of finishing. Then I set a tentative date for termination, usually several months ahead. I may take advantage of a coming vacation or necessary separation, and use that event as the target, so that the end doesn't seem like an arbitrary and cruel severance. Then I wait for the reaction.

HOUSEWIFE: What reaction? You mean you know in advance something is going to happen just because you set a date?

PSYCHOANALYST: I know it. But the patient doesn't. Very often, no matter how prepared he has felt for termination, no matter how beautifully he has learned to deal with his emotions, as soon as the end of our relationship becomes a living possibility, he collapses. In various ways he unconsciously protests against the separation—his old symptoms return, his mistaken attitudes reappear, he retrieves his used, worn-out resistances from the junk heap.

HOUSEWIFE: Maybe it's frightening to think of being on your own after all the years of depending on the analyst.

PSYCHOANALYST: Quite so, and the patient shows his conflicting feelings about it. Ellen, for instance, dreamed at this point in her analysis, that she was a little girl—the child of a friend—riding a bicycle up the steep hill in front of their home. At first she couldn't control it, and it swerved frighteningly from side to side, and even circled backward, but at last she did get it under control, and rode it to the top of the hill, where her mother—actually Ellen's real friend—was watching in the doorway. She got off the bicycle and burst into tears, feeling immense relief at having arrived safely but furious with her mother for having let her go through the agony of the experience.

As she talked about the dream afterward, she spoke of the admiration she consciously had for the child's real mother, Ellen's friend. This woman, she said, loved her child dearly, but allowed her great independence, instead of being tearful and overprotective, as Ellen's own mother had been. Then she interpreted the dream herself, saying that I was the mother, and that she wouldn't allow herself to admit the respect she felt for me, nor the control which she was gaining over her life, as over the bicycle. But she acknowleged that the dream admitted that she wanted to succeed, as she had indeed done.

CAREER GIRL: Sounds as though she wasn't too badly off. But you said that many of the problems reappear; what do you do about them?

PSYCHOANALYST: We must resolve them all again. This time, however, it's much easier. I am more active in dealing with the patient, and he is much less defensive and much wiser and more understanding. Many an analyst eases the patient into independence by making the sessions less frequent, too, or expressing personal opinions, so that, instead of the anonymous analyst, he gradually becomes the individual he really is. And the patient usually accepts the idea. He begins to bring different kinds of problems to the analyst. Carla, toward the end of her analysis, would discuss furniture and the location of the home and the size of the wedding she and her fiancé were planning. She would ask my opinion as though I were simply a friendly man, and one who might well help her know what her fiancé would like.

HOUSEWIFE: Then you do end on the date you propose?

PSYCHOANALYST: Close to it. There are times when termination has to be postponed for several months, but an analyst doesn't usually propose a date if it's not feasible.

CAREER GIRL: Isn't it terribly painful, even if you're well, to leave the analyst, after years of such closeness?

PSYCHOANALYST: There is certainly a bittersweet quality to the parting, for both the analyst and the analysand. Nor is the patient's reluctance to end completely pathological. He feels—and should feel—genuine affection and gratitude. In fact, many patients find in the analytic relationship the first friendly and healthful contact of their lives; and until enough time has passed for them to develop other friendships, it may well be the only one.

HOUSEWIFE: But you don't become friends with your patients, do you?

PSYCHOANALYST: The majority of analysts consider such a practice unwise—after all, the patient may need to come back in a year or two or five, and if friendship has intervened, he won't be able to. There are some analysts, however, who stipulate that, after a waiting period of perhaps six months or a year, an ex-patient can call as a friend. This is to allow time for any remnants of the analytic dependency to disappear.

TEACHER: Does it always disappear? Does every patient accept the dissolution of that special relationship? Aren't there ever unsuccessfully treated people who are never willing to drop their analysts?

PSYCHOANALYST: Unfortunately, there are. It's a rather common reason for failure in analysis. The patient substitutes a wish to be treated for a desire to be cured. He never becomes emotionally sturdy enough to walk alone. I know of one case—it cannot even be called a real failure—in which the patient has been under treatment with various analysts for over twenty years. The man originally was unable to walk out of the house; his parents had to support him; he had no life whatsoever. Now he is earning a large income, has a home of his own and a kind of social life with other people. No one would deny that he has greatly improved; but he falls apart without his steady visits to his analyst, developing anxiety attacks which paralyze his functioning. Hopefully, the matter will be resolved, but even if it isn't, he is getting a needed and useful effect from unending analysis, as a diabetic does from daily doses of orinase or insulin.

TEACHER: Is that what Freud meant by "interminable analysis"?

PSYCHOANALYST: That's one of the possibilities he discusses in "Analysis, Terminable and Interminable," one of his later papers. You see, not infrequently, when it is clear that the analysis has reached a stalemate and no progress has been made for months and months, the analyst must decide whether discontinuing the sessions will do more harm than good. Further, the majority of analysts would agree, I think, that in an absolute sense analysis is always an interminable process. That is, it is a never-ending education, because life is a never-ending progression of events and changing roles. The difficulty is in deciding at what point the analysand is able freely to assume the task of analyzing his own behavior and can continue to learn on his own.

LAWYER: You've spoken as though the analyst makes all the decisions. Doesn't the patient ever figure he's had enough and quit?

PSYCHOANALYST: Indeed he does. Sometimes a patient improves enough to be benefiting from his neurosis and finds he wants nothing more. One of my patients, a clothing contractor, learned to use his aggressions in his work. He was no longer inactivated, as he was when he first came to analysis, by an immobilizing fear of leaving his room. He had turned his hostility outward successfully enough. But instead of ridding himself of it in analysis, or learning to use it constructively, he shifted it into a driving competitiveness. Our society, alas, bestows financial awards on such a trait, but it made a hell on earth for his employees and associates. However, he was unwilling to make any further effort to change his character. He was freed from pain, and successful to boot, and not surprisingly, he was satisfied. Often patients aren't willing to stand the frustration and anxiety necessary to take them past such a point.

LAWYER: You haven't mentioned any outright failures; surely such cases exist.

PSYCHOANALYST: I fear they do. Analysis, after all, attempts to treat a large variety of emotional and mental ills, and can't be expected to achieve the same ratio of success with all of them, any more than medicine does with such widely differing diseases as diabetes, cancer, and diphtheria. There are bound to be analyses which are unsuccessful, especially when measured by our optimal goals.

LAWYER: Maybe, then, some patients are more realistic than their analysts, and are right to settle for less than the shiny new character you hold out for them.

PSYCHOANALYST: Perhaps. On the other hand, sometimes it is the patient whose desires are the too lofty and even unattainable ones. A patient often feels that analysis has failed because he still has, clutched to his breast, the expectations which he brought with him when he entered treatment. Like a child who expects to see Houdini and gets instead only a book on how to do card tricks, he's dissatisfied because he isn't magically and effortlessly cured; he still has problems which he is expected to solve himself, he still faces frustrations, and he hasn't become universally beloved. We analysts try to be realistic. We say the patient should be *capable* of more meaningful relationships and effective functioning. But he can only develop his powers in terms of his own education and life circumstances. We can't hope to make a successful construction engineer out of a middle-aged man who could never pass high school math, though we rid him of all his self-doubt and inhibitions. But though we try not to look for miracles, and don't expect to remove *all* anxiety or guilt feelings, we would like the patient to feel guilt only for the wrongs he has actually committed, to have him make amends for those wrongs, if possible, and to learn to bear up under his feelings when nothing can be done about them. For the courage to bear pain is a true sign of maturity.

TEACHER: How long does it take to learn to behave maturely? You said Carla's analysis took over five years. That's quite a protracted piece of education.

PSYCHOANALYST: Is it, really? When a patient has spent the first twenty-five years of his life learning the wrong way to act, relearning can't be accomplished via a fast, snap course. Nor is it possible to predict the length of an individual analysis. We do know that the changes in character which are the present-day goals of psychoanalysis take a good deal longer than the elimination of symptoms, which was its goal in its early years.

LAWYER: Surely there are figures which show the average length of treatment, aren't there?

PSYCHOANALYST: I can tell you what the average training analysis is in this country, and that's considered complete, of course. It averages four to five years, or about seven hundred hours. And a survey in Great Britain made among practicing analysts indicates their training analyses averaged eight hundred hours. But for lesser goals, for improvement rather than cure, which is frequently all that is possible, and all that a patient wishes for or can manage financially or emotionally, two or three years is probably closer to average.

TEACHER: What do you mean by "improvement"?

PSYCHOANALYST: Most of us define genuine improvement as the point where the patient's symptoms are alleviated; where he now functions, though he once could not; or where, if he functioned poorly, he now does notably better; where, providing fate doesn't throw him a wicked curve, he will get along with himself and his society. And still, it is possible that he may relapse under some new stress, for such a patient hasn't gone far enough along in the slow re-educating process of analysis to have strong protection against future troubles.

TEACHER: But how does improvement differ, then, from the reparative psychotherapy you told us about earlier?

PSYCHOANALYST: Reparative psychotherapy guides the patient into more productive activity without attempting to uncover the repressions which influence his behavior. It tries, too, to give him enough self-awareness to reduce his internal conflicts, and he can often learn new patterns of behavior from such help. Analysis, on the other hand, attempts to remove the unconscious resistances to healthful patterns of behavior, so that the patient can understand and control his actions, whatever his circumstances. A man who has received short-term psychotherapy has been set on a path through a forest. If he stays on the right road, he's fine. But should he come to a fork in the road, he's not so well off as the fellow who has a map to indicate the way. This man with the chart, of course, is like the analyzed person with his insight. And, if I may carry the analogy a bit further, a grizzly bear might unexpectedly chase either of them off the path completely, and then the importance of a detailed plan of the whole forest becomes obvious.

CAREER GIRL: How many analysands learn to read their charts, simple or detailed? Or, if I may leave the forest, how many analyses are considered successful?

PSYCHOANALYST: As I said, profound character change is a relatively new goal, and there aren't enough statistics available for an adequate judgment of complete change. But reports of analysands "cured or improved" generally hover about the two-thirds mark, and some run considerably higher.

TEACHER: What proportion of these patients stay well?

PSYCHOANALYST: Most analysts, unfortunately, aren't in a position to answer that question. The nature of the relationship, that of the individual patient with a therapist in private practice, precludes an objective follow-up study. The therapist hasn't the time, the man-power, or the moral right to launch an investigation into the lives of his former patients. Of course, an analyst keeps records of returning patients, and he may be able to draw some conclusions by new interviews with any he can find after a number of years, but it proves very little statistically, since each analyst treats probably no more than 150 individuals in a lifetime of practice.

There is more information on miscellaneous psychotherapeutic treatment, since a good deal of it is conducted in institutions. And since most of such treatment is partly derived from psychoanalytic concepts, I can properly use the findings for illustration. Indeed, much that is called psychotherapy might be called psychoanalysis by any but the orthodox Freudian's definition. At any rate, the general conclusion is that the more the therapy deals with the unconscious forces, the more lasting the effect.

LAWYER: That's a little vague. If I'm to judge your cause, I'd like to hear more precise figures.

PSYCHOANALYST: Statistics are tricky things, especially in this field. Let's defer examining them in detail until the next time we meet.

CHAPTER NINE

IT'S HERE TO STAY

Analysis compared to other therapies; the meaning and non-meaning of statistics; Freud's influence on our lives, in sickness and in health; the effect of psychoanalysis on the sciences; the promise of the future.

LAWYER: I've been looking forward to the evidence of your statistics, Doctor, because I still have some doubts. I read a report which showed that the same proportion of cases improve with ordinary medical treatment from their family doctor as do with psychoanalysis. This report was based on five hundred consecutive disability claims made on the Equitable Life Assurance Society, all cases of one kind of neurosis or another. The claimants were all unable to work, and in fact, the three months they were laid up was a prerequisite for filing a claim. But they were all treated only by general practitioners, in their own fashions, not by formal psychotherapy, and within two years over 70 percent had returned to work and stayed well enough to continue for at least five years.

PSYCHOANALYST: Yes, I'm familiar with the P. G. Denker report. It compared those treatment figures with summaries of other studies of neuroses which had been treated in other ways.

LAWYER: Right. And those summaries covered reports of over a thousand cases from a number of hospitals and clinics which gave psychiatric treatment, and also approximately the same number of cases from still other sources which offered psychoanalysis. What I found amazing—and amusing—was that the figures, regardless of the kind of treatment or the source reporting results, were pretty much the same—between 60 and 70 percent got better.

PSYCHOANALYST: Before you laugh too loudly, I must tell you that there are grave weaknesses in the report. For example: exactly what was wrong with the patients in the several studies used? After all, some illnesses disappear spontaneously while others are comparatively resistant to treatment, and unless the people getting different kinds of treatment had comparable kinds of illness, the comparison is quite invalid. Again, what standards of recovery were used by the G.P.'s to judge the improvement of the Equitable patients, other than the fact that patients were able to return to their jobs and to get along? Such a "recovered" patient could be going to work compulsively, facing the ordinary daily decisions with uncalled-for anxiety and gulping aspirin and tranquilizers for his nervous headaches; or he could be fighting with his teen-age daughter so constantly that she elopes at sixteen; or he could indeed have recovered spontaneously—as one would expect—from a temporary depression that had been caused by the death of his wife.

LAWYER: But the psychiatric and psychoanalytic treatments reported on produced similar proportions of good results. Why was that?

PSYCHOANALYST: I've already explained that figures from short-term psychotherapy cannot be equated with those of psychoanalysis, because the *goals* are so different. The goals of the reparative psychotherapist, in the outpatient psychiatric clinic, are admittedly far less ambitious than those of the psychoanalyst. As for hospitalized patients, there are additional, and differing, factors which may influence treatment, such as the relief from home stresses, the therapeutic attitudes of the various attendants, and the contacts with new people.

Here's just one indication of how limited the Denker report is, and how impossible it is to form adequate judgments from studies which lump figures together in this fashion. One of the studies summarized by Denker is by R. P. Knight. This study itself is a composite one covering almost one thousand cases previously reported, which had been treated by psychoanalytic therapy, and it concludes that the figures for success on all the cases average about 66 percent—which doesn't sound much better than any other form of therapy. Yet Dr. Kenneth Appel, a leading psychoanalyst, notes elsewhere that if you extract from Knight's data the cases which were treated more than six months, you'd find an improvement rate for that group of 92 percent.

TEACHER: I find it difficult to believe that Equitable would base its payments for mental illness on nonpsychiatric evidence, anyway.

PSYCHOANALYST: That report was published close to twenty years ago. I imagine the company has quite different regulations today.

TEACHER: Do you know what standards and figures are used today by the insurance companies which cover mental illness?

PSYCHOANALYST: I don't know on what figures all insurance companies base their plans, but Group Health Insurance used a pilot program to work out its arrangements, depending in large part on the evaluation of the twelve hundred participating psychiatrists. These doctors sought, they said, improvement, not complete recovery, and they found that the short-term therapy they offered resulted in the "improvement or recovery" of 75 percent of their patients. Incidentally, the fact that insurance companies now recognize psychotherapy, and pay claims for psychotherapeutic treatment, is probably the *ne plus ultra*, the final proof of its acceptance in America. And indeed, many major medical policies and Blue Shield and Blue Cross plans, as well as the Group Health Insurance, now offer coverage for emotional illnesses, including payments for group therapy, psychological tests, visits to private psychiatrists' offices, and up to a month of treatment by a psychiatrist in a general hospital.

TEACHER: Psychotherapy may be accepted, but nevertheless I read a disturbing report, which can't be discounted simply because there are still no well-defined standards. A single psychiatric clinic gave interviews and one of the standard psychological tests to an unspecified number of applicants for therapy. Although one hundred and fifty applicants were judged in need of help, about twenty-five, arbitrarily chosen, had to wait six months until a clinical worker was available. At the end of the six months, all one hundred and fifty were given the psychological test again, and all of them—including the twenty-five who only waited—

showed improvement! What's more, they all showed approximately the same amount of improvement. How do you explain that?

PSYCHOANALYST: Let me say first that I know of a similar study in which the untreated patients did *not* improve. I think the whole point is quite moot, at this juncture; research is clearly inadequate. But simply considering your report, and arbitrarily accepting its data, I can think offhand of a number of factors which might explain the results. One is the questionable validity of the test: there is no psychological test known today which all by itself can provide the basis for really sound judgments. Another factor is the short period of time involved—too short to prove very much of anything about the effectiveness of psychotherapy. And the third point is the fact that all these people might have felt themselves in the hands of capable authority— even those who had not yet begun treatment—and this does have some effect.

TEACHER: Could that be all you need? Perhaps if the patient is sicker, he may need more time, and that's why the analyst, whose treatment extends over a longer period, may seem to help people who can't be reached otherwise. Or perhaps the crux of the matter may be the figure of authority who's present in all these cases: the family doctor, the psychiatrist, the psychoanalyst, or the psychotherapist. The mere existence of the substitute father may be the real curative factor.

LAWYER: And what the analyst does may not be the reason at all for the patient's recovery!

PSYCHOANALYST: No one has ever proved that causality is more than an accepted way of looking at a repeated sequence of events. Yet everyone—the scientist included—acts on an assumption of causality all the time. And in analysts' offices all over the country thousands of patients every day see and feel the cause-and-effect of psychoanalysis. Each of them is familiar with the subtle yet specific changes that take place after some long, tense silence has been broken, or a disturbing dream analyzed, or a seemingly unfathomable rage accounted for. Perhaps rigorous scientific proof of the superior value of psychoanalysis isn't available yet, but the value itself is unquestionable.

LAWYER: But maybe the improvement would have come anyway, in time. All these surveys may only prove that time is the factor that really counts.

PSYCHOANALYST: It's true enough, that, given time, the self-healing process operates in a considerable number of cases of minor or externally caused psychological disturbances. But in all too many others, where external stress plays on internal weakness, people get no better, or even worse as time goes by; some neuroses, like some physical diseases, are simply too strong for the individual's self-healing capacities. There is, indeed, for some a grave danger of eventual breakdown in delay, while prompt action might have avoided it. One of the reasons for the remarkable change in recovery figures from modern mental hospitals is the recognition that speed of action is of utmost importance. At the better hospitals, up to 85 percent of newly admitted patients have been leaving within six months after entering; less fortunate souls, who have been there for many years, and arrived before the new treatment methods existed, are imprisoned inextricably in their illness. As with psychosis, so too with neurosis —the sooner treatment is begun, the more effective it is.

LAWYER: I concede that you've given us a lot of logical reasons why analysis is *probably* of value, but surely there must be some way to find out scientifically and rigorously just how good it is?

PSYCHOANALYST: Yes, but it's difficult—perhaps even impossible in its present state. Dr. Lawrence Kubie, a leading psychoanalyst, long ago pointed out that in order to carry on any systematic evaluation, the results reported by the individual patient and his private therapist would have to be supplemented by data from subsidized treatment and foundation-backed studies. This work would have to include not only the well-to-do, but people from every social and economic class, and every part of the country. Only thus could the significance of a man's cultural background and economic circumstances be adequately examined.

CAREER GIRL: And we could see why the rich get neuroses and the poor get psychoses.

PSYCHOANALYST: Among other preconditions, though, we'd have to agree upon definitions of illness and cure, and each treated patient would have to be matched with another ill person, similar in background and symptoms, who received no treatment, and with still another person, similar in background, who was normal at the outset of the study. And, as if that weren't enough, in order to compare one method of therapy with another, these conditions would have to be duplicated for each therapeutic process.

CAREER GIRL: But *all* these people might think they felt better, or that they were making progress onward and upward through life. Most of us feel that way.

PSYCHOANALYST: We wouldn't go solely by the subjects' judgment. Far from it. There would be a broad body of information and data, including the results of not-yet-perfected psychological tests, and the observations and evaluations of many observers of the patients and the nonpatients. From all this, the conclusions would be drawn by teams of professional people, including clinical psychologists, sociologists, and social workers, as well as psychotherapists from various schools of thought.

LAWYER: That's a tall order.

PSYCHOANALYST: Yes, it is. But until such desirable cooperation takes place and definitively measures the value of the psychotherapies, I believe we're justified in continuing to use what techniques are available to us. After all, the cure rate for lung and stomach cancers by surgery is estimated at only 5 to 15 percent, but no one suggests that such operations be dropped. I'm sure we do a great deal better than that, even if our success rate is well below 100 percent.

TEACHER: Yes, compared to the rest of medicine, you hold your own very nicely. And even aside from psychoanalysis as a therapy, I must say I'm tremendously impressed with the effects it has had on our society. I don't suppose any single scientific theory has so affected us. Wasn't it W. H. Auden who said it created a whole climate of opinion? A great deal of what we think and feel, whether we're aware of it or not, is colored by Freud's discoveries.

HOUSEWIFE: Oh, yes! I can see it among my friends. We automatically excuse one woman for her nasty tongue because we know she's unhappily married, and we're all very concerned about bringing up our children so that they'll be well adjusted.

CAREER GIRL: I have my doubts, sometimes, about all that concern. I'm not trying to deny Freud, or even Spock, but I can remember the period—luckily now past—when my friends, smiling wanly, would apologetically remove the pillow Sissy was using to smother Baby, guilt-ridden that they had already scarred Sissy's tender little psyche by having Baby at all.

LAWYER: Psychoanalysis has brought us a new life, all right, for better or worse. I must say I welcome a psychological war, no matter how chilling, in preference to being involved in actual shooting. After all, as the saying goes, you could get killed there. On the other hand, I don't care to have a sports car sold to me on the strength of my secret desire for a mistress, or possibly-cancer-producing cigarettes urged on teen-agers as a road to beauty, love, and springtime. In fact, I'd gladly give motivational research back to the Madison Avenue Indians.

TEACHER: There have certainly been some unforeseen results of psychoanalytic discoveries and their acceptance in popular thinking. In an essay called "Theology and Self-awareness," recently published in England, the Rev. Harry Abbott Williams, Dean of Trinity College, Cambridge, in England, makes a point that must seem startling to many people. Speaking of the necessity of accepting Freudian thought, he cites two movies, *Never on Sunday* and *The Mark*, to demonstrate that fornication is not always unchristian. He points out that in *Never on Sunday* a prostitute gives herself to a young, nervous sailor in such a way that he gains self-respect and confidence, and Dean Williams declares that to be an act of Christian charity. As for *The Mark*, he believes that since the cure for the protagonist's abnormality —his sexual desire for children—is initiated by his illict intercourse with an accepting woman, her action is a healing, and therefore Christian, one, too.

CAREER GIRL: Yes, I'd say psychoanalysis had arrived. Even articles about movie stars have to be slanted to show how emotionally disturbed they really are, deep down under. Who would ever have thought that Hollywood starlets would be required to have not just well-filled sweaters, but pain-filled psyches?

PSYCHOANALYST: Even the federal Civil Service Commission has been affected. Jobs are being made available to more people with a history of mental illness. A news item reports that the Commission has discovered how ideally suited some neurotics are to particular jobs—a withdrawn person as a librarian in a Government agency, or a chronically ill man who desires solitude on a high-security job, working alone from midnight to dawn in a semideserted building, for instance. The obsessive-compulsives who cannot tolerate discrepancies, in fact, are considered perfect for positions like that of mail clerk, which require meticulous attention to detail. But not only the Civil Service Commission has recognized the force of the unconscious. Courts, prisons, juvenile agencies all over the country, whether city, state, or federal, all use or want help of one kind or another in our field, either for testing or for treatment. One state now has on its payroll more than sixty psychiatrists and psychologists who give therapy. It's no wonder that thirteen thousand psychiatrists and more than eighteen thousand psychologists aren't enough for this country.

CAREER GIRL: But there are already family service agencies, child guidance clinics, social workers and counselors in school, mental health clinics, hospital outpatient psychiatric clinics, even traveling mental health units. What hath Freud wrought?

PSYCHOANALYST: All the facilities now in existence, however, can only treat about one-tenth—some two million—of the twenty million or more psychologically disturbed Americans. The goal proposed by the Joint Commission on Mental Illness and Health is to have one fully staffed, full-time, mental health clinic serving every fifty thousand people—or more than double the present number of such clinics. So you can see that Freud's influence is still widening. In fact, whole new sciences have grown out of his discoveries, and the established ones have been enormously altered. Psychiatry before Freud was little more than a static labeling of illnesses; now the knowledge of how the unconscious forces operate offers a dynamic approach to the field. Moreover, psychosomatic medicine never before existed as a science, and the more organized psychosomatic studies didn't begin until the late 1920's; today it is well established as a special study, and widely practiced. Even in areas which are still considered the province of organic medicine, the importance of the emotions is increasingly admitted today.

HOUSEWIFE: I read that a dentist in Australia even did a study recently to show that after times of severe emotional strain people's teeth seemed to decay more.

CAREER GIRL: That fortress of organic medicine, the hospital, doesn't seem to have been invaded by any brave new reasoning. Its attitude toward the patients still seems pre-Freudian to me.

PSYCHOANALYST: That's far from correct, I'm glad to say. Psychotherapy is an important adjunct to the treatment of patients who are in hospitals for other reasons. Social workers employed by the hospital quite routinely now have interviews with new patients in order to determine their mental state, and offer them reassurance and comfort for whatever ordeal they face. These workers will see the patients' families, too, and act as emotional interpreters for them and the patients, when it's useful. In a great many hospitals today, every person on the staff is aware of the demons in a man's mind, and the torment they can inflict.

HOUSEWIFE: Are you talking about *all* hospitals or just mental hospitals?

PSYCHOANALYST: All good hospitals have modified their practices in accordance with these psychological facts of life. Mental hospitals today, of course, use many techniques which have grown out of the knowledge of psychoanalytic theory. Occupational therapy, although its benefit was known to the ancient Greeks and Egyptians, is proving enormously effective because of our understanding of the nature of repressions. Doctors, using the technique as a bridge to a creative, healthy use of one's drives, will prescribe the job which seems indicated—some simple, repetitive task to relieve anxiety, for example, or noisy, vigorous work to alleviate hostility. Thus in a hospital's woodworking shop one patient might paint plywood fish for a mobile, while another might sandpaper a magazine rack, and still another might carve a statue of a warrior—and each activity would not be haphazardly chosen, but selected in accordance with ideas stemming from dynamic psychology. The same principle is used in recreational therapy. Games, which are so often battles in disguise, are chosen to afford the best type of competitive outlet for each patient's aggression. Punching bags and golf balls with names and faces of hated relatives—or the psychiatrist—are encouraged to release repressed anger. The pastime of fingerpainting is offered for the obsessively clean people.

HOUSEWIFE: I thought fingerpainting was supposed to be for children because they enjoy getting dirty.

PSYCHOANALYST: Yes, it allows them to do a forbidden thing. Another "forbidden thing" is acting out, which, though not encouraged by psychoanalysts for *their* patients, is a boon to psychiatrists for the psychotics who can't put their problems into words. In fact, psychodrama—a refinement of "acting out"—is a burgeoning outgrowth of the need for modified treatment based on psychodynamic principles for those who can't or won't accept psychoanalysis itself.

CAREER GIRL: Isn't a psychodrama a real play, with a plot and actors and an audience?

PSYCHOANALYST: It can be. As used by Dr. J. L. Moreno, who developed the technique, there is a real stage, on which the patient acts out, or watches others act out, a personal problem, and the therapist helps the patient choose the problem, selects the other players, suggests the action, and guides a follow-up discussion between the audience and the members of the cast. But there are less formal and elaborate uses of it, too, not only in hospitals, but in all kinds of institutions, as well as among ordinary groups of neurotics, people with marital problems, pregnant women, and the like.

HOUSEWIFE: Is that considered group therapy?

PSYCHOANALYST: It's one kind of group therapy. A much more common example is of a group of people who discuss their problems together, under the guidance of a psychotherapist. Besides being used in hospitals, group therapy is used in outpatient clinics, child guidance centers, schools, private offices, prisons, churches, and even business establishments. In the therapeutic sessions, each patient receives understanding and respect from the others, learns to communicate emotionally with them, and finds himself able to talk about his troubles, secure in the acceptance of the group. Under the skilled supervision of the therapist, who helps to untangle any emotional obstacles along the road, the patient learns better ways of behaving toward the rest of the world.

TEACHER: Has this kind of treatment been found to be as effective as privately conducted psychoanalysis?

PSYCHOANALYST: Group therapy is quite effective for certain kinds of patients. Whether it can accomplish as much as individual analysis is still a debated point. Moreover, not everyone is accessible to such treatment, and its use with the kind of neurotic patient who comes to psychoanalysis has so far been rather limited. But a number of those patients have recently been going into "combined therapy," where they see the same therapist in group and in individual sessions; this works quite well in some cases. Generally speaking, the practitioners of group therapy, of whom there are estimated to be between two and three thousand today, are enthusiastic about their field. It would certainly be a more feasible way of helping a great many more people.

LAWYER: Group therapy and psychodrama sound like good bets for what were once called "reform schools."

PSYCHOANALYST: Many ramifications of psychoanalytic concepts are used in correctional institutions, and with noteworthy results. The Kansas Boys' Industrial School, for example, recently reported the results they had achieved by trying to understand why the boys act as they do and by helping them to correct their maladjustments. Thirty years ago, they said, forty out of every one hundred youths released eventually were sent back. Today the ratio has dropped to eight out of one hundred.

LAWYER: I guess the verdict is in your favor, Doctor. You've presented a convincing case. And now, before you step down from the witness stand, would you care to make a statement about the future plans of your profession?

PSYCHOANALYST: I think the future of psychoanalytic therapy is clearly charted. Beginning with Freud himself, psychoanalysts have been experimenting with new techniques toward a more effective and economical treatment method. Group therapies, or fewer, more widely spaced individual sessions, or more active participation by the analyst via new techniques of response to the patient are several of the present directions some of us are exploring. A synthesis of psychotherapy with drugs which are not yet known is another avenue of possibility. I feel confident that many methods for better treatment will be evolved, and that the next generation will bring even greater cooperation between psychoanalysis, the physical sciences, such as biology and physiology, and such social sciences as anthropology and sociology. And the aim of all the workers in these fields will be not only the cure, but the prevention of mental illness.

In the meantime, we analysts will continue to do what every doctor does—that is, attempt to ease the suffering of other men. I'm really very proud that psychoanalysis offers more than nepenthe—more than oblivion for pain and sorrow. It offers a knowledge and understanding of the psyche and its unconscious processes which can help human beings, as can all knowledge, to become masters of themselves and their environment, to love one another, and perhaps thus to approach that most elusive goal of all—happiness.

APPENDIX A

MORE ABOUT SOURCES FOR SIMPLE OR REPARATIVE PSYCHOTHERAPY AND ITS NONANALYTIC PRACTITIONERS

Many an individual is troubled by problems which affect his relationships with other people, and his behavior at work, at home, or with his friends; or he feels depressed, nervous, anxious, or uneasy without any adequate reason; or he believes himself to have some of the symptoms described in Chapter III. Yet he may remain unsure about the need to consult a psychoanalyst, or feel a great reluctance to do so. For such a person, a visit to a family service agency, pastoral counseling center, or mental health clinic is an ideal beginning. Such organizations can offer diagnosis and, if it is required, referral to a qualified psychoanalyst, but the counseling and palliative psychotherapy they provide are, in many cases, sufficient to relieve the disturbance which brought the patient there in the first place.

THE TYPES OF TREATMENT CENTERS

Family service agencies are usually under the direction of, and staffed primarily by, social workers; almost all are operated on a voluntary basis, about 90 percent of their income being from United Fund and Community Chest contributions. They handle practical problems such as the placement of children in foster homes and marital difficulties, as well as many emotional illnesses. More than 300 such agencies—mostly nonsectarian—are affiliated with the Family Service Association of America. Through these affiliates about 2,600 social workers see some 700,000 people a year. There are other agencies, not so affiliated, which do more or less similar work; the Family Service Bureaus of the Salvation Army and the Family Service Departments of Catholic Charities are the best known.

Over 100 *pastoral counseling centers* have appeared within the last decade. They are usually staffed and run in much the same way as family service agencies, and clergymen especially trained in counseling are available, along with a variety of other counselors and psychotherapists.

The 1,600 *mental health clinics* presently in operation in this country serve an estimated 450,000 people a year, and are more thoroughly distributed, geographically speaking, than the family service agencies. Mental health clinics, whether state-, federal-, community-, or privately controlled, are under the supervision of psychiatrists. They can therefore deal with the more serious neuroses, some of the psychosomatic complaints, and even some psychoses, and may prescribe and dispense drugs. The majority of patients are seen, nevertheless, by social workers and clinical psychologists, and receive the less intensive forms of psychotherapy.

THE PEOPLE IN THESE AGENCIES

Most of the 20,000 *social workers* who have received a master's degree from an accredited school of social work, and have had special training in counseling, work for the above-mentioned agencies. (About 2,000 offer similar services in part- or full-time private practice.) Within the agency or clinic setting, the social worker can treat many emotional problems; consult, as a member of a team, with other specialists; and, when confronted with an emotional disorder requiring techniques beyond simple or palliative psychotherapy, he can make referrals to the appropriate sources.

Clinical psychologists who work for these clinics and agencies hold at least a master's degree, or more often a Ph.D., in psychology, and have had training in diagnostic psychological testing or psychotherapy, or both. They may offer guidance, counseling, and deeper forms of psychotherapy to clients with a large variety of psychological disorders, but not those caused by or resulting in physical ailments. They also often administer and interpret psychological tests. There are about 6,000 clinical psychologists practicing today, a large number of whom are connected with these organizations.

As to *clergymen,* only a very small number of the approximately 9,000 who have had some training in counseling make their services available at pastoral counseling clinics. Most of those clergymen who have been adequately trained through one of the more than 200 special programs in pastoral counseling and psychology use their knowledge exclusively for the benefit of their own parishioners.

Roughly a fifth of the 13,000 *psychiatrists* presently practicing in the United States spend all their time in clinics, hospitals, or social agencies. Those who do are, of course, trained and authorized to diagnose and treat even the most severely disturbed patients; to deal with any mental or emotional problem including those with physical causes or complications; and to prescribe and use drugs and other somatic therapies. Psychiatrists may or may not be able to practice psychoanalysis; even if they are, they do not do so in these clinics.

THE FEES CHARGED IN AGENCIES AND CLINICS

In no matter what agency or clinic, the surroundings are about like those in a doctor's or lawyer's office, and the patient is treated with the same degree of privacy; but the fees are considerably lower than those of a private practitioner. Fees may vary somewhat from agency to agency, and they do tend to be higher in the larger metropolitan areas, but most of these centers and clinics base their charges on the patient's ability to pay. These charges may range from nothing to as much as $25 an hour; very few people pay the top fee, however. The average mental health clinic has a ceiling fee of $10, and most of its patients pay considerably less; a typical Family Service Association affiliate charges between $7 and $10 an hour for a family of four with a take-home pay of from $7,500 to $9,000.

LOCATING A TREATMENT CENTER

To find an agency, center, or clinic near you:

a) the simplest and safest thing to do is to call your local mental health association, listed in the telephone directory either as "(Your County) Mental Health Association" or "Mental Health Association of (Your County)." Most of the 900 chapters and divisions of the National Association of Mental Health have directories of approved local mental health facilities, and all of them should be able to offer names of nearby agencies which will give you advice, diagnosis, and therapy.

b) If there is no local mental health association, call the United Fund, Community Chest, or Department of Public Welfare in your community. These, too, should be able to supply the desired information.

c) Try the classified telephone directory. Even the most respectable-sounding name, however, is not a guarantee of reliability. There is no legal restriction on such names as "Child Guidance Clinic" or "Marriage Counseling Center," and the organization bearing such a name could be staffed by poorly trained or even dishonest people. Look first, therefore, under "Family Service Association of America," or one of the similar organizations mentioned above, for the names of the local agencies actually affiliated with these groups.

Because psychological symptoms are even more apt than physical ones to be misleading, and because they are particularly difficult for the sufferer to recognize and understand, you can do nothing better, if you are in emotional distress, than to go to one of the above-described treatment centers as a first step. None will overcharge you or try to retain you as a patient when you are no longer in need of them; nor are they likely to hold on to you if your illness is beyond their scope.

APPENDIX B

GUIDEPOSTS TO A REPUTABLE ANALYST

If you insist on finding an analyst on your own, or through the recommendation of a friend, rather than in the more reliable ways suggested in Chapter V, you should at least make sure that he is a member of one of the recognized professional associations, and that he has received his analytic training from an institute with adequate standards. Chapter V offers directions for ascertaining such information; below are lists of reputable organizations and training centers, association with which is a good indication of a practitioner's ethics and education.

PROFESSIONAL ORGANIZATIONS

This list does not include local groups, no matter how worthy, nor does it, even on a national basis, claim to be definitive. The lack of over-all organization or legal discipline in the field of psychoanalysis makes it necessary to rely on reputation rather than on hard-and-fast regulations. Nevertheless, the few associations which are named are known to have high standards for membership.

The organizations which admit only psychoanalytic psychotherapists are few. The major one, of course, is the American Psychoanalytic Association (which admits only physicians who have been trained as analysts at one of the training institutes approved by it). In alphabetical order, they are:

ACADEMY OF PSYCHOANALYSIS
125 E. 65th Street, New York 21, N.Y.

AMERICAN PSYCHOANALYTIC ASSOCIATION
1 E. 57th Street, New York 22, N.Y.

ASSOCIATION FOR APPLIED PSYCHOANALYSIS
103 E. 86th Street, New York 28, N.Y.

ASSOCIATION OF PSYCHOANALYTIC PSYCHOLOGISTS
c/o Nathan N. Stockhamer, Ph.D., 103 E. 86th Street, New York, 28, N.Y.

COUNCIL OF PSYCHOANALYTIC PSYCHOTHERAPISTS
c/o Jacob Nussbaum, Ph.D., 315 Central Park West, New York 25, N.Y.

NATIONAL PSYCHOLOGICAL ASSOCIATION FOR PSYCHOANALYSIS
26 W. 9th Street, New York 11, N.Y.

There are a number of other excellent professional associations, which are not limited to psychoanalysts but to which analysts often prefer to belong. Although the simple fact of membership in one of them will not demonstrate that a member is a practicing analyst, the history of his training and experience and his current status can be secured from the association. These broader-spectrum associations include:

AMERICAN ACADEMY OF PSYCHOTHERAPISTS
30 Fifth Avenue, New York 11, N.Y.
AMERICAN ORTHOPSYCHIATRIC ASSOCIATION
1790 Broadway, New York 19, N.Y.
AMERICAN PSYCHIATRIC ASSOCIATION
1700 Eighteenth Street N.W., Washington 9, D.C.
AMERICAN PSYCHOLOGICAL ASSOCIATION
1333 Sixteenth Street N.W., Washington 6, D.C.

TRAINING CENTERS

Once you have ascertained an analyst's connection with a reputable association, and have found out where he was trained, make sure his training was received at an institute with high requirements, including his own and control analyses. The list presented here is, again, limited. It is impossible to site all the adequate training programs—they are simply not known.

The nineteen institutes under the jurisdiction of the American Psychoanalytic Association are listed first and separately. Training in them would indicate an orthodox background, which may, of course, have been altered by experience. They are listed because, as mentioned in Chapter V, analysts may have received their training at one of these centers, although, not being psychiatrists, they have not been admitted to the American Psychoanalytic Association.

BALTIMORE PSYCHOANALYTIC INSTITUTE
BOSTON PSYCHOANALYTIC SOCIETY & INSTITUTE
CHICAGO INSTITUTE FOR PSYCHOANALYSIS
CLEVELAND PSYCHOANALYTIC INSTITUTE OF THE SCHOOL OF MEDICINE, WESTERN RESERVE UNIVERSITY
COLUMBIA UNIVERSITY PSYCHOANALYTIC CLINIC FOR TRAINING AND RESEARCH
DIVISION OF PSYCHOANALYTIC EDUCATION, STATE UNIVERSITY OF NEW YORK

INSTITUTE OF THE PHILADELPHIA ASSOCIATION FOR PSYCHOANALYSIS
LOS ANGELES INSTITUTE FOR PSYCHOANALYSIS
MICHIGAN PSYCHOANALYTIC INSTITUTE
NEW ORLEANS PSYCHOANALYTIC INSTITUTE, INC.
NEW YORK PSYCHOANALYTIC INSTITUTE
PHILADELPHIA PSYCHOANALYTIC INSTITUTE
PITTSBURGH PSYCHOANALYTIC INSTITUTE
SAN FRANCISCO PSYCHOANALYTIC INSTITUTE
SEATTLE PSYCHOANALYTIC TRAINING CENTER
SOUTHERN CALIFORNIA PSYCHOANALYTIC INSTITUTE
TOPEKA INSTITUTE FOR PSYCHOANALYSIS
WASHINGTON PSYCHOANALYTIC INSTITUTE
WESTERN NEW ENGLAND INSTITUTE FOR PSYCHOANALYSIS

The following two schools are exclusively for physicians, but differ in their theoretical orientation. The first follows the teachings of Karen Horney, and the second is eclectic.

AMERICAN INSTITUTE FOR PSYCHOANALYSIS
NEW YORK MEDICAL COLLEGE

Below are the institutes which offer training programs for both physicians and nonphysicians. As you can see by the names, not all can be called analytic in the Freudian sense, but they are reputable, and are therefore named. Those with an asterisk do not specify in their literature their requirements for personal and teaching analyses, but are presumed to have them nevertheless.

INSTITUTE FOR PSYCHOANALYTIC TRAINING AND RESEARCH
NATIONAL PSYCHOLOGICAL ASSOCIATION FOR PSYCHOANALYSIS
NEW YORK SOCIETY OF FREUDIAN PSYCHOLOGISTS*
POSTGRADUATE CENTER FOR PSYCHOTHERAPY*
SULLIVAN INSTITUTE FOR RESEARCH IN PSYCHOANALYSIS
TRAINING GROUP FOR CLASSICAL PSYCHOANALYSIS*
WILLIAM ALANSON WHITE INSTITUTE

INDEX

A

A. A. (Alcoholics Anonymous), 46
Abraham, Karl, 64, 78
Acting out, 131-132, 157
Action for Mental Health, see Joint
Commission on Mental Illness and
Health
Addicts, 44-46
Adler, Alfred, 77-78, 80
Aggressive drive, 70-71
Alcoholics, 45-46
American Medical Association, 89-90
American Psychoanalytic Association, 85-86, 88
American Psychological Association, 89, 90
American Psychologist, 84
Anal phase, 63-65
Analysand, *see* Patient
Analysis and Analyst, *see* Psychoanalysis and Psychoanalyst
"Analysis, Terminable and Interminable," 143
Anna O., case of, 57-59
Anthropology, and psychoanalysis, 79, 159
Anxiety, dreams, 112-113; lack of, in character disorders, 44-47; neurosis, 41; and neurotic symptoms, 5, 37-38, 41, 43-44
Appel, Kenneth, 150
Associations for psychoanalysts, 84-90; listed, 164-165

B

Benedict, Ruth, 79
Bernheim, Hyppolyte, 59
Beyond the Pleasure Principle, 70

Bleuler, Eugen, 77
Bonime, Walter, 114
Breuer, Josef, 57-59
Brill, A. A., 50, 111
British Psychoanalytic Society, 87

C

Castration fear, 67-69
Catharsis, 20, 59, 121
Change of life reaction, *see* Involutional psychosis
Character, development, 34-35, 63-76; disorder, 44-48; reconstruction, 9, 136-137
Charcot, Jean Martin, 57
Civil Service Commission, 154-155
Clergymen, as psychotherapists, 19-21, 161-162
Clinical psychologists, *see* Psychologists
Combat neurosis, 19
Community Chest, 161, 163
Compulsion, 35-36, 38
Conscious and unconscious processes, 31-35, 106-108
Conversion hysteria, *see* Hysteria
Cornell Medical College, 49
Council of Psychoanalytic Psychotherapists, 87
Countertransference, *see* Psychoanalysts, attitude toward patient
Creativeness, and psychoanalysis, 11
Culturally Deprived Child, The, 39
Cure, *see* Improvement

D

Darwin, Charles, 56
Death instinct, 70

167

About the Authors

While the research and writing of *The Talking Cure* took a year, the book reflects the accumulated experience of many years on the part of all three authors. MORTON M. HUNT has studied and written about psychology for a dozen years. A 1941 graduate of Temple University, Mr. Hunt's work for a Master's degree at the University of Pennsylvania was interrupted by wartime service in the Air Force. For some time an editor for *Look* and *Science Illustrated*, Mr. Hunt has been a free-lance writer since 1949. His range of subject matter is extraordinarily wide, but he writes most often on the behavioral sciences. Mr. Hunt is a regular contributor to *The New Yorker*, and his work has also appeared in national magazines such as *Redbook, Harper's* and the *Saturday Evening Post*. He is the author of three books—*The Natural History of Love, Her Infinite Variety*, and, most recently, *Mental Hospital*.

RENA CORMAN's byline has appeared in the *Saturday Evening Post* and the *New York Times Magazine*. She is responsible for much of the special research which went into this book, including the reading of scores of books and over a hundred magazine articles, interviews with spokesmen for the American Psychiatric Association, the American Psychoanalytic Association, the Council for Psychoanalytic Psychotherapy, leading analysts, and many individuals who had undergone analysis. Married and the mother of a son, Mrs. Corman has collaborated with Mr. Hunt on several earlier books and articles, and is presently at work on a book of her own.

DR. LOUIS R. ORMONT is a graduate of four universities and studied with Theodore Reik and Hyman Spotnitz, among others. He also attended several analytic institutes, taking the bulk of his training with the National Psychological Association for Psychoanalysis. Entering private psychoanalytic practice in 1952, he also worked in various clinics, including the Madison House Psychiatric Clinic. On the faculty of Columbia University Teacher's College since 1958, he is a member of the American Psychological Association, the New York State Psychological Association, American Group Psychotherapy Association, and several other professional organizations.

Format by Anne Hallowell
Set in Linotype Caledonia
Composed, printed and bound by American Book-Stratford Press, Inc.
HARPER & ROW, PUBLISHERS, INCORPORATED

Date D...